THE LUFTWAFFE BATTLE OF BRITAIN FIGHTER PILOT'S KITBAG

UNIFORMS & EQUIPMENT FROM THE SUMMER OF 1940
AND THE HUMAN STORIES BEHIND THEM

Also by Mark Hillier:

Westhampnett at War

To War in a Spitfire

Joe Roddis: In Support of the Few

*Suitcases, Vultures and Spies: From Bomber Command to Special Operations
The Story of Wing Commander Thomas Murray DSO DFC**

*A Fighter Command Station at War: A Photographic Record of RAF Westhampnett
from the Battle of Britain to D-Day and Beyond*

War Birds: the Diary of a Great War Pilot

*The RAF Battle of Britain Fighter Pilot's Kitbag: Uniforms & Equipment from
the Summer of 1940 and the Human Stories Behind Them*

THE LUFTWAFFE BATTLE OF BRITAIN FIGHTER PILOT'S KITBAG

UNIFORMS & EQUIPMENT FROM THE SUMMER OF 1940
AND THE HUMAN STORIES BEHIND THEM

Mark Hillier

FRONTLINE
BOOKS

THE LUFTWAFFE BATTLE OF BRITAIN FIGHTER PILOTS' KITBAG
Uniforms & Equipment from the Summer of 1940 and the Human Stories Behind Them

Mark Hillier

First published in Great Britain in 2018 by Frontline Books,
an imprint of Pen & Sword Books Ltd, Yorkshire - Philadelphia

Copyright © Mark Hillier, 2018
ISBN: 978-1-47384-995-2

The right of Mark Hillier to be identified as Author of this work has been asserted by him in accordance with the Copyright, Designs and Patents Act 1988. A CIP catalogue record for this book is available from the British Library All rights reserved.

No part of this book may be reproduced or transmitted in any form or by any means, electronic or mechanical including photocopying, recording or by any information storage and retrieval system, without permission from the Publisher in writing.

Typeset by Aura Technology and Software Services, India
Printed and bound in India by Replika Press Pvt. Ltd.

Pen & Sword Books Ltd incorporates the imprints of Pen & Sword Archaeology, Air World Books, Atlas, Aviation, Battleground, Discovery, Family History, History, Maritime, Military, Naval, Politics, Social History, Transport, True Crime, Claymore Press, Frontline Books, Praetorian Press, Seaforth Publishing and White Owl

For a complete list of Pen & Sword titles please contact
PEN & SWORD BOOKS LTD
47 Church Street, Barnsley, South Yorkshire, S70 2AS, UK.
E-mail: enquiries@pen-and-sword.co.uk
Website: www.pen-and-sword.co.uk

Or

PEN AND SWORD BOOKS,
1950 Lawrence Roadd, Havertown, PA 19083, USA
E-mail: Uspen-and-sword@casematepublishers.com
Website: www.penandswordbooks.com

CONTENTS

Introduction	vii
Acknowledgements	ix
Note on Images	x
Section 1: Flying Helmets	1
Section 2: Oxygen Masks	18
Section 3: Goggles	23
Section 4: Flying Clothing	30
Section 5: Lifesaving Equipment	48
Section 6: Service Dress	74
Section 7: Other Flying Equipment and Paperwork	120
References	136
Bibliography	137

THE LUFTWAFFE BATTLE OF BRITAIN FIGHTER PILOT'S KITBAG

INTRODUCTION

I have always been interested in the events of the Battle of Britain and the aircrews on both sides who took part, but my personal focus is in the human story not the chronology or squadron histories. What was it like for the young fighter pilot during that period, what was the equipment like and what difficulties did the crews face? Having studied the story of the RAF with regards its development and issue of equipment, it was also my desire to do the same thing with the Luftwaffe kit, and compare and contrast the two.

The questions that I was keen to find answers for included, were they more technologically advanced, had they thought more about the equipment required for the fighter pilot of the day and was that equipment fit for purpose? It is obvious from the established research already carried out that certainly the Luftwaffe had thought long and hard about the flying equipment they had issued to their crews and they certainly had much more to choose from, even considering different types of equipment for different climates, with summer and winter flying suits, for wear over water and land. They had also had chance to use the equipment in anger and learn from their experiences during the Spanish Civil War and the Blitzkrieg through Poland in 1939. This is particularly clear for example when you look at the flying goggles used by the Luftwaffe, which pretty much centred around three types honed and developed from experience, whereas the RAF took quite a while and numerous types, developed throughout the war, to end up with a good set of goggles fit for most purposes.

What is clear is that the Luftwaffe fighter pilots certainly went for a more dashing, if you like, look compared to their RAF counterparts, with their leather jackets, riding breeches and top boots or jackboots, looking like they were ready to mount their steed and ride into action. Often kit was worn against standing orders but for the fighter pilots this was often overlooked.

The RAF pilots were more reserved and stuck to smaller statement-pieces of individual uniform adjustments mainly for practical reasons like the silk scarf, that served a purpose. The only showmanship, if you like, was the unbuttoning of the top button on the tunic to signify a fighter pilot. The Luftwaffe pilots and crews were also supposed to remove their metal awards and flying badges before operations, yet many PoW photos show Luftwaffe crews being rounded up in the south of England wearing both. It was thought that the metal flying badges and any sharp edges might cut or penetrate the life jacket, rendering it useless.

What has become apparent when looking at the uniforms and equipment used by both sides in the conflict is that most actually preferred to wear uniform, partly due to the hot summer, when flying as described by Oberleutnant Hans Theodor Grisebach of 2/Jagdgeschwader 2: 'it was a lovely summer's day when we took off on an escort mission over Portsmouth. It was so warm, all I was wearing was a shirt, blue trousers, flying boots with flares strapped to the top, a flying helmet and life jacket. I also carried a pistol.'[1]

THE LUFTWAFFE BATTLE OF BRITAIN FIGHTER PILOT'S KITBAG

This book does not focus on the day-to-day life of ground crew and aircrew with the cut and thrust of the operations of the period, the emphasis is instead on the aircrew uniform, and equipment issued to them or privately purchased and how it was used. With this is mind I have produced a photographic archive specific for the Battle of Britain period which can be used as a reference for collectors, modellers and aviation buffs alike.

I have chosen to limit the kit to that which was used, issued or purchased by those Luftwaffe aircrew who flew fighter aircraft such as the Bf 109 and Bf 110. The equipment shown in the following pages is typical of that available to the aircrew between the official dates of the Battle which are recognised as 10 July 1940 to 31 October 1940. What must be noted is that in the eyes of the Germans the Battle continued through the Blitz until June 1941. Where I have included kit that was used late in 1940 or 1941 I have explained its inclusion or where it is difficult to pinpoint an exact date for example.

By 1941 items such as the *kanal hosen* or Channel trousers and suits with a multitude of survival gear was by then starting to become standard issue. I have not included many items from the period after October–November 1940 although I have indicated where some kit may have been introduced prior to June 1941 although again issue dates and availability are often not clear cut. The *Battle of Britain Kit Bag* starts with the headgear worn, working down to flying clothing and equipment and then lastly uniform and insignia and paperwork.

What has been clear through handling and researching the Luftwaffe equipment is that is almost all equipment is clearly labelled and most items including awards, badges and wound badges even have maker's identification. There are some exceptions to the rule and of course privately-purchased items are hard to date.

I have used established guidance and references from authors such as Brian L. Davis, Roger James Bender and Mick Prodger who have spent many decades trying to decipher records, yet sometimes they too admit to struggling to produce a definitive answer on dates. There have been many myths and legends over the years about Luftwaffe kit and I have considered long and hard before adding some items. I have made up my own mind from established first-hand accounts and photographs where dated, taking note of established texts and where I have taken a move from these references I have given my reasoning. Obviously sometimes this can lead to errors but where doubt exists I have also expanded on this in the text and in some cases it's an educated guess.

The book sets out to place pictures of items within private collections alongside period photos and it is hoped that this guide will give enthusiasts a basic pictorial reference to the equipment used during that specific period. It is not designed to be an all-encompassing reference, which has been done previously by other authors. This kit bag will bring to you a snapshot of concise information about the equipment used in just that small window of the war and in the Luftwaffe case, demonstrate how varied the kit was compared to that used by the RAF.

Mark Hillier,
Fontwell, West Sussex, 2018.

ACKNOWLEDGEMENTS

Without the established research and work carried out by Mick J. Prodger, as well as his support, this publication would not have been possible. At the same time, the expertise and guidance of experienced collectors such as Simon Lannoy, Ken Aitken, David Farnsworth, Paul Woodbyrne and Phil Phillips, who have given their valued time and knowledge, has been invaluable. Thanks must go to my long-suffering wife Kate and children Molly and George for their continued support. Chris Goss has also been invaluable in helping with period photographs and for allowing me to make extensive use of quotes from his excellent books - without which the human element of the items shown would have been harder to reveal. Thanks to Greg Percival for the help with photography. Lastly thanks to Martin Mace for encouraging me to produce the book.

NOTE ON IMAGES

All of the items that appear in this book are held in private collections and have been acknowledged accordingly. Please note that much of the equipment is both rare and fragile, with the result that it has not always been possible to obtain the best presentation or angle during the photography.

Section 1
FLYING HELMETS

The Luftwaffe had available to them three types of flying helmet, depending on the climate or temperature, as compared to the RAF with only the B Type leather flying helmet. The Luftwaffe authorities and the manufacturers had realised that the purpose of the flying helmet had changed somewhat since the early days of open-cockpit flying when the helmet was offering protection against the elements. The design criteria were now focused on the helmet being a comfortable fit and to enable free movement as well as ensuring that the acoustic quality of the earphones and microphone were not compromised. Regarding the oxygen supply, the priority was to ensure that it was free flowing when needed at altitude and that it did not pull off of the face during high G manoeuvres. So its securing to the helmet was of key importance.

All of these helmets featured utilised the throat-type microphone whereas the RAF had chosen a microphone within the oxygen mask. The helmets were categorised into three basic types: those made of linen for use in a warm climate which carried the designation 'S' for '*Sommer*', those made of leather and lined with lamb's wool for colder climates which carried the designation 'W' for winter and lastly a lightweight helmet constructed with net panels for use in very hot climates or weather which had the designation 'N' for '*Netzkopfhaube*'. In this book I have concentrated on the flying helmets fitted for radio communication that were mainly in use during the Battle of Britain.

The Luftwaffe had also spent a considerable amount of time on research into the development of oxygen masks. There were two main models issued pre Battle of Britain, both fitted well and had a three-strap system which ensured a good fit and chamois leather interiors to help a tight fit against the face and provide some comfort. The early masks from the 1930 period unfortunately proved prone to freezing at higher altitudes due to the moisture being exhaled. The Luftwaffe went on to produce a fighter mask model with two straps and a heated range of masks to prevent freezing as well as a non-heated, non-freezing mask in 1939 which was particularly popular.

Regards goggles, it was appreciated that pilots still needed protection to prevent dust in the eyes, flying fragments and insects but they had issues that needed to be overcome to ensure the pilot could maintain optimum vision for tactical advantage. All goggles could be prone to fogging up and optical deficiencies, amongst other issues. Early on the Luftwaffe realised that the interaction and fitting between the flying helmet and the goggles was also important. As a result the LKp S and W 101 series of helmets incorporated a moulded notch for retaining the strap of the flying goggles, ensuring a better fit. Interestingly some models also had tinted lenses to aid with looking for enemy aircraft in the sun, essential for a fighter pilot who had to have a swivel neck and eyes on stalks to

THE LUFTWAFFE BATTLE OF BRITAIN FIGHTER PILOT'S KITBAG

ABOVE: A typical Battle of Britain flying helmet setup of an early LKp S 100 with aluminium domed ear pieces, three-strap 10-67 oxygen mask and Model 306 *Fliegerschutzbrile* goggles. (Mick Prodger Collection)

FLYING HELMETS

gain the upper hand in combat. As a comparison the RAF Mk IIIa goggles did not have this option and only later models of the RAF goggles carried flip-down shades.

FLYING HELMET MODELS LKp W100 AND LKp S100

Essentially these two helmets were the mainstay for aircrews in the Battle of Britain, both having the provision for earphones and throat microphones. The summer-weight flying helmet is constructed of a tan-coloured linen material and normally is found with a slate-grey synthetic satin-type lining. The winter weight is constructed to the same essential pattern but from dark brown goat's leather with

ABOVE LEFT is shown the LKP S100 (summer weight) version of the classic flying helmet showings its domed aluminium ear phone cups distinctive to this version. Note the throat microphone preferred by the Luftwaffe. This also has a three strap 10-67 oxygen mask very typical of the period. (Mick Prodger Collection)

ABOVE RIGHT is the same helmet worn with the Model 306 goggles. The throat microphone was not without its issues and if too tight could cause the wearer some discomfort if too tight and if too loose, poor communication! (Mick Prodger Collection)

ABOVE: A clearer image of the flying helmet on its own showing the top triangular connection for the middle strap of the oxygen mask and the throat microphone arrangement. These flying helmets are the iconic versions which you will see in period Luftwaffe photos. (Simon Lannoy Collection; www.themilitariadealers.com)

FLYING HELMETS

ABOVE LEFT: Here is the winter version of the LKp 100 flying helmet. Of leather construction this time but essentially the same pattern with lamb's-wool lining for comfort at altitude or low temperatures. Exactly the same connection points for the three-point oxygen mask and the same throat microphone. Again photos of this variant exist from the Battle of Britain period. (Paul Woodbyrne Collection)

ABOVE RIGHT: The early round throat microphone on the LKp W100 flying helmet with its connector lead and plug for the radio. Although this style of microphone was the mainstay of the Luftwaffe flying helmets, it was not ideal and could be uncomfortable if too tight. (Paul Woodbyrne Collection)

THE LUFTWAFFE BATTLE OF BRITAIN FIGHTER PILOT'S KITBAG

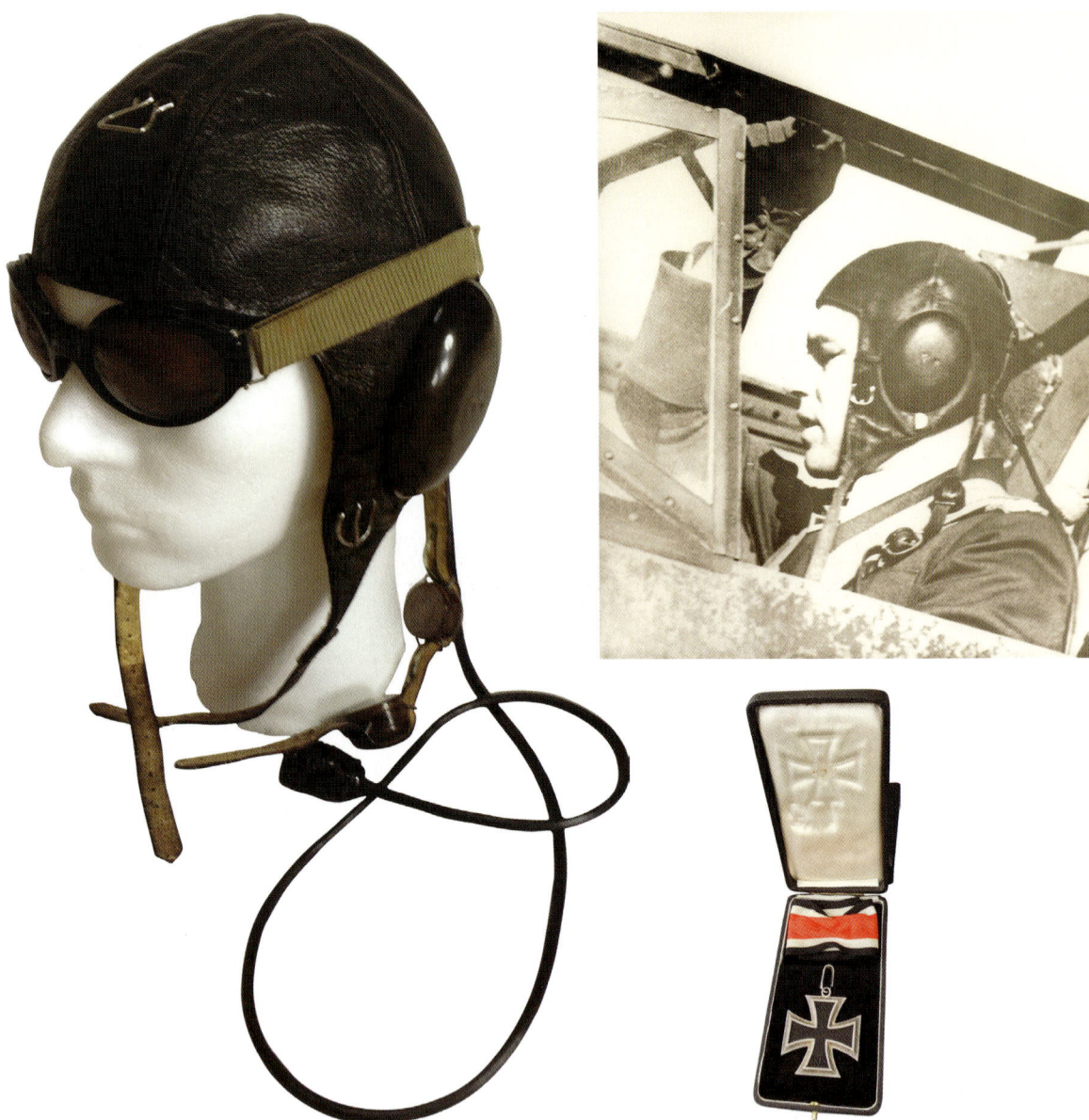

ABOVE LEFT: The LKp W100 flying helmet again, worn with the early second pattern Model FL.30550 *Splitterschutzbrille* flight goggles with the solid bridge, illustrating the fact that the goggles do not sit on the earpiece very well and ride up, especially when pulling G in combat! (Paul Woodbyrne Collection)

ABOVE RIGHT: Hauptmann Helmut Wick of 1/Jagdgeschwader 2 in the cockpit of his Bf 109E-4. Note he is wearing an LKp W100 helmet and the Knight's Cross which he was awarded on 27 August 1940. He would be awarded the Oakleaves to it on 6 October 1940. Rather than issue leather flying gloves he is wearing his officer's dress gloves. He was killed in action on 28 November 1940. (Chris Goss)

BELOW RIGHT: A boxed Knight's Cross of the Iron Cross, the same as that awarded to Helmut Wick on 27 August 1940. This example was manufactured by Juncker. (Ken Aitken Collection)

FLYING HELMETS

RIGHT: The front cover of *Helmut Wick: Das Leben eines Fliegerhelden* which, published in two different versions by the Luftwaffe magazine *Der Adler*, the first being in 1943, carries an excellent portrait of Wick. He can be seen wearing his *Schirmmutze* (or uniform peaked cap), this one showing the typical 'saddle form' of the period, and a *Tuchrock* (or service tunic with the silver officer's piping to the collar). Wick is also wearing the Knight's Cross with Oak Leaves around his neck. On his tunic button is the ribbon of the Iron Cross Second Class, which he gained in 1939. On his chest is the 'Sudenetenland' medal ribbon. The Flying Badge and Iron Cross First Class would be worn on the left breast pocket, but these cannot be seen in this portrait. The collar badges show the rank of Major with the gold yellow *Waffenfarbe* of flying personnel. (Historic Military Press)

BELOW: Internal view of the LKp S100. (Paul Woodbyrne Collection)

THE LUFTWAFFE BATTLE OF BRITAIN FIGHTER PILOT'S KITBAG

a white lamb's wool lining. Both helmets have brown domed aluminium protective cups over the earphones which are iconic to the period concerned.

Internally both had the earphone surrounds covered in lamb's wool to help prevent undue pressure on the wearer's ears. Too much pressure on the head on long flights would cause a headache. Both had two snap fasteners on leather straps externally at the rear which held the goggle elastic in place. They were secured to the head by the use of dual chinstraps and these were buckled to the helmet on either side.

The oxygen mask was connected to the helmet by a single hook on each side of the face, just under the protective cover to the ear and then a single non-elasticated strap and slide buckle up and across the nose to the forehead where the mask was held in place by a triangular hook which was connected to a short length of adjustable strap. This ensured a good fit of the mask over the nose and mouth.

FLYING HELMET MODELS LKp S AND LKp W101

These models were essentially identical in materials to the 100 series, with the winter variant being lined with lamb's wool, the principal difference being the construction of the earphone housings. On the 101 series the earphones were of moulded dark-brown leather. The earphone cover also differs in that there is a notch in the side of it for retaining the goggles in position as shown in the photographs. These were available from 1938 and had improved earphones for radio communication and were a vast improvement on the 100 series. Again, all of the flying helmets are well marked internally with maker, model and often date.

LEFT: A summer LKp 101 helmet showing the sculpted earpiece allowing the better fit of the goggles. Note the helmet retained the three fixing points for the oxygen mask. This and its winter variant had much better electronics for improved communications and were available after 1938. (Paul Woodbyrne Collection)

FLYING HELMETS

LEFT: This is the LKp W101 model flying helmet, available from 1938 onwards. Constructed of leather, and this one lined with rabbit fur, although mostly they were lined with lamb's wool. These had improved receivers over the LKp W100 version but similar fixings and adjustments. They are shown with a later pair of clear-lens Model FL.30550 *Splitterschutzbrille* flight goggles, which have the hinged bridge connection. (Phil Phillips Collection)

RIGHT: This photo shows in more detail the round throat mike receivers which indicate an earlier helmet. The four-pin connector for the radio can also be seen. (Phil Phillips Collection)

ABOVE: This is the LKp W101 with the eyelets and studs for attaching the 10-69 mask, shown here being worn. Fighter pilots preferred this type of set-up with the two-strap oxygen mask fixing. This and the LKp S100 with eyelets and studs were quite prevalent at the beginning of the war. (Mick Prodger Collection)

FLYING HELMETS

ABOVE: Here a Bf 110 pilot runs up the engines on his aircraft prior to a sortie. He is wearing an LKp S101 flying helmet with sunglasses and a seat-type parachute. (Chris Goss)

RIGHT: This Unteroffizier poses for a photograph behind a Bf 109 cowling. He is wearing an LKp S101 helmet. Note the clip above his nose for a three-point oxygen mask. (Mark Hillier)

ABOVE: The front cover of the 9 January 1940 edition of *Der Adler*, the Luftwaffe's in-house bi-weekly magazine. The image depicts a youthful Bf 109 pilot being strapped into his cockpit by his groundcrew. He wears a KW33 one-piece winter flight suit, which was often worn in the early part of the war for winter flights, but not during the Battle of Britain due to being too bulky and cumbersome for summer use. However, the flying helmet shown is a summer LKp S101 helmet with leather-covered ear cups, which are sculpted to help retain the goggle strap. These were introduced into service in 1938 and, along with the earlier LKp S 100 model, were commonplace during the Battle of Britain. The goggles he is wearing are the Model 295. (Historic Military Press)

FLYING HELMETS

FLYING HELMET MODEL LKp N101 LIGHTWEIGHT NETTING HELMET

The idea behind this flying helmet was that it would be cooler for pilots in the summer or flying in tropical climates. It was designed to take the earphones, throat microphone and to support the oxygen mask but it offered little or no protection to the wearer as its upper panels and crown were just a dark-brown cotton netting or mesh. This style of helmet was favoured by the fighter pilots as it

LEFT: This image shows the LKp N101 flying helmet on its own. This is an earlier two-point connection helmet or first pattern favoured by the fighter pilots with a long 1m lead. Note also the domed studs for the two-strap 10-69 oxygen mask attachment. The net gets very fragile and often these have been repaired, as has this one. They are very difficult to find with early dates; it is thought these were introduced in mid-1941 but some photos as shown in this book indicate that these may have been available slightly earlier, towards the end of the Battle of Britain. (Mark Hillier Collection)

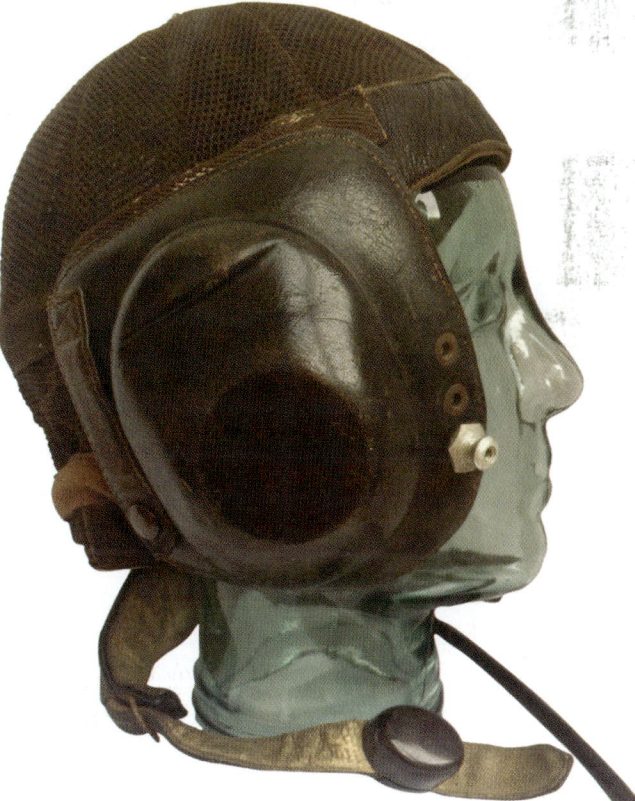

RIGHT: A side view of a LKp N101 flying helmet. (Mark Hillier Collection)

THE LUFTWAFFE BATTLE OF BRITAIN FIGHTER PILOT'S KITBAG

ABOVE: An LKp N101 flying helmet with the double-strap configuration and a helmet cover which helped keep the pilot's head cool, but also aided recognition if he was shot down. The helmet is seen here with a Model 1067-01 oxygen mask, which, a much later design, was not available during the Battle of Britain.

FLYING HELMETS

ABOVE: Oberleutnant Anton Stangl of 5/Jagdgeschwader 54 in the cockpit of a Bf 109E-1/E-3 wearing an LKp N101 lightweight netting helmet and sunglasses. Note the metal stud on the side of the helmet specifically for the attachment of the 10-69 or 10-6701 fighter pilot's mask with the two fixings. Stangl's favourite aircraft number was Black 14. Indeed, he was flying Bf 109E-4 coded Black 14, Wk Nr 1277, when he collided with another aircraft over Kent on 1 September 1940. He baled out and was captured with his kill total standing at six. (Chris Goss)

BELOW: Seen here wearing a LKp N101 lightweight netting helmet is the Battle of Britain pilot Claus Rene Wouters. He was killed in action within days of the end of the Battle in early November 1940. Note the domed stud for connection of the 10-69 oxygen mask with two-point connection. (Chris Goss)

THE LUFTWAFFE BATTLE OF BRITAIN FIGHTER PILOT'S KITBAG

was quick to put on and cooler to fly in. Again, the earphone housings were constructed in the same way as those of the LKp 101 series, although this helmet also had an additional strap with a snap fastener to help hold the goggles in place. The two-fixing model without a clip on the forehead pre-dated the three-fixings version for the three-strap oxygen mask. The official date of the introduction of the N model is thought to have been the summer of 1941, but photographs exist of it being worn by fighter pilots in the Battle of Britain. I have included a photo of a casualty of 1940 wearing the N model. I certainly feel these were available in late 1940, if not in limited numbers prior to this date. The difficulty is that there appears to be none that survive in collections having relevant dates so photographic evidence is all that is available.

FLYING HELMET COVER

These helmet covers come in a variety of colours. The main ones for the European theatre were white, red or yellow and were of simple cloth construction often with hooks for attachment to the helmet. Some were also secured by the goggle retaining straps. The types varied depending on the helmet type, some sculpted to fit around the ear and some pulled over the ear cups. They served two functions, one to keep the head cool in the glazed cockpit which would have been like an oven in the summer, the other to help spot downed pilots from above when in the Channel. The Luftwaffe had a better-organised air-sea rescue service than the RAF and had floatplanes, buoys and patrol boats to help rescue downed crews.

RIGHT: Shown here are two variants of helmet covers. The top example has a brown cotton weave and yellow interior, the other a red exterior. The brown one has hooks to connect to the helmet, whereas the red is elasticated. (Phil Phillips Collection)

FLYING HELMETS

ABOVE: A propaganda image from 1940 depicting Oberleutnant Carl-Alfred Schumacher. He is wearing a summer flying suit, LKp S101 flying helmet and helmet cover.

Section 2
OXYGEN MASKS

A huge amount of research was carried out by the Germans on the use of oxygen masks prior to the Second World War and the masks in use during the Battle of Britain were superior to those of the RAF. One of the main problems encountered by the crews with the early HM-5 and HM-15 masks was ice in the expiratory valve which was caused due to the moisture of the exhaled air freezing. This would mean that the pilot would only be breathing in normal air and before long would suffer from hypoxia.

Many pilots and crew lost their lives to this as it was not easy to recognise the onset of symptoms due to the fact that the sufferer became quite happy and dozy, losing concentration and eventually passing out. The Luftwaffe masks are much lighter in weight than their RAF counterparts but were only used for the supply of oxygen and did not contain a microphone for communication as the Germans adopted the throat-type microphone. The main types seen in use during the period had either the three-strap fixing, which clipped on to the helmet across the face and vertically across the bridge of the nose, and the two-strap variety which only fixed across the face. The latter type was favoured by the fighter pilots as they were quick and easy to put on and take off. All of the masks were fitted with a standard 'quick-disconnect' system which would release it from the aircraft at a set pull force, essential for those bailing out of an aircraft in a hurry. The masks vary in colour and manufacture and it would not be possible to cover all the variations but only to mention the principal types used.

Some of the Luftwaffe aircrew arriving to replace losses in the Battle of Britain often had very few hours in the air and had not even flown on oxygen and used the masks as described by Ulrich Steinhilper 'Typical of these youngsters who arrived in late September [1940]. His flying time was minimal – he had only fired a few shots at a ground target, had never flown on oxygen and still had no idea how to use his radio.'[2]

MODEL HM-5 AND HM-15 OXYGEN MASKS

This pre-war mask was available in two sizes, the smaller being designated the HM-5, but they are exactly the same. Its distinguishing features being the three straps to secure it to the flying helmet and its 'T'-shaped sealing frame, constructed of rubber with a chamois leather interior to make it warmer and more comfortable to wear. To a degree this also prevented frostbite at altitude as it covered the cheeks and chin. The idea of the three straps was that the head strap supported the weight of the

OXYGEN MASKS

mask and the oxygen hose, while the side straps tightened the mask against the face to give a good seal. Again the hose was fitted with a quick disconnect which had been developed by the Luftwaffe early in the 1930s. This mask had one drawback in that it was prone to freezing when the exhaled moisture-laden breath hit the cold flow of the oxygen, causing ice to form in the supply hose and expiratory valve. Some crews of larger aircraft carried spare masks with them in case of freezing. By the time of the battle these masks could be found in use but had been superseded by the 10-67.

MODEL 10-69

One disadvantage of the HM-5 and 15 was they were not easy to fasten or take off in a hurry due to the three strap fastening. Fighter pilots preferred the 10-69 mask which was produced in four sizes. This mask was available as early as 1937. Although it was essentially the same in design as its predecessors, it had a simplified two-strap fixing and was predominantly used with a stud fixed to

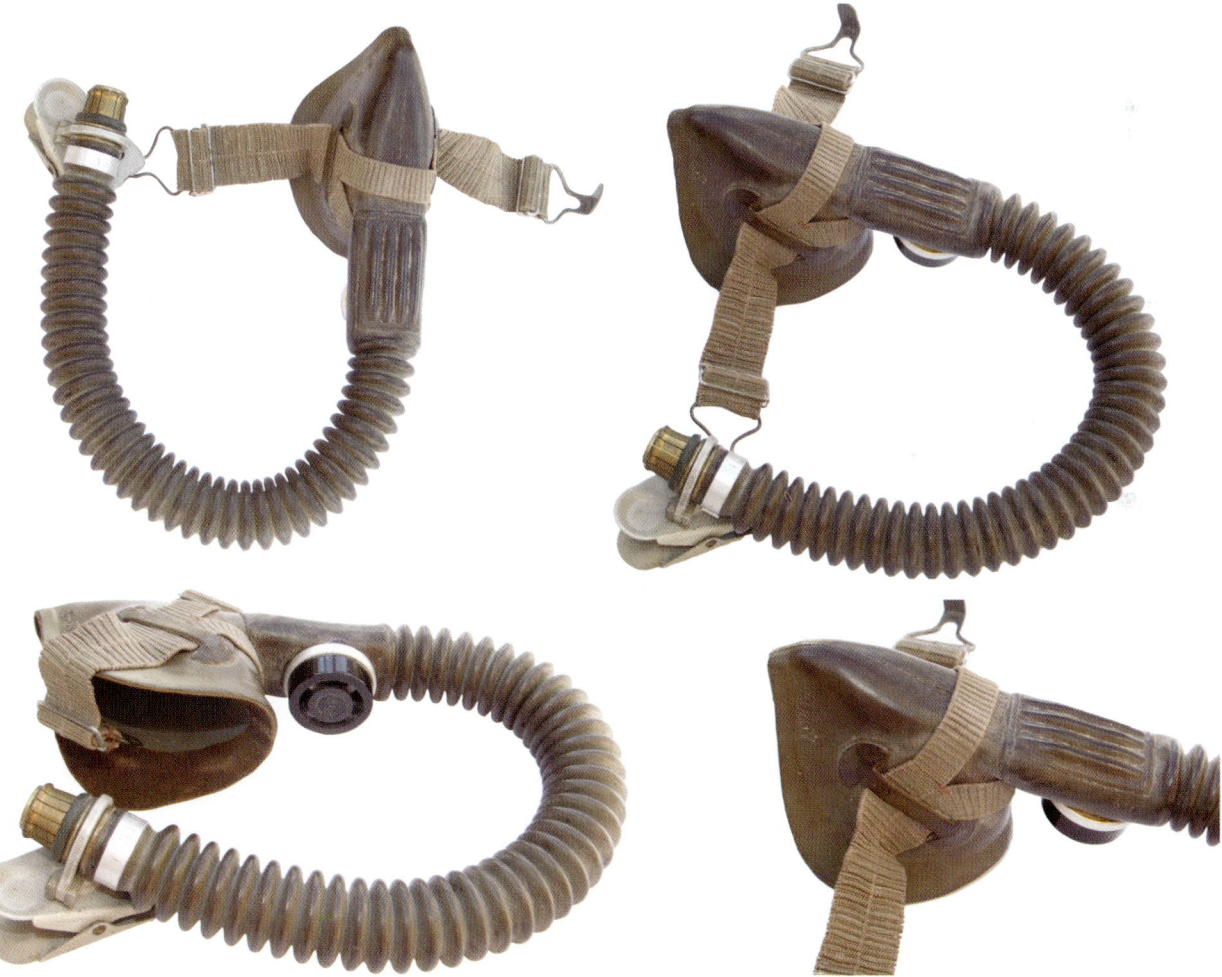

ABOVE: A series of shots showing the 10-69 Model mask with two fixings as favoured by fighter pilots. Almost identical in style to the earlier Hm5/15 with the same ribbed front. Note the exhalation valve on the back of the pipe. (Phil Phillips Collection)

ABOVE: A close-up of the 10-69 oxygen mask showing its attachment to the LKp W101 helmet. Of interest are the domed studs which aided a quick connection. (Mick Prodger Collection)

OXYGEN MASKS

LEFT: A selection of fighter pilots' equipment at dispersal of 3/Jagdgeschwader 53, Le Touquet, October 1940. Visible are a LKp W101 helmet with metal studs for the attachment of a 10-69 mask, a Kapok life jacket, and a seat-type parachute. To the rear are two dye marker packs to aid with search and rescue if downed in the sea. (Chris Goss)

the helmet on each side. Later these were standard on the LKp N101 helmet. The mask could be worn hanging on one side and fixed very quickly back across the face, taking only a few seconds to do if required. It was light and comfortable and hence more popular than the other varieties. The problem of freezing in the supply line was still an issue, however. Several attempts were made at electrical heating to prevent freezing but these were not very effective.

MODEL HM-51, ALSO KNOWN AS THE MODEL 10-67

This mask was available from 1939 and was principally designed to try and eliminate the risk of freezing. Some improvements were made in the design and a twin-wall lower portion of the mask was constructed to provide some insulation. Other improvements were made in the expiratory valve. It was very similar in look to the earlier HM-5 and HM-15 with a three-strap system to secure it to the flying helmet.

RIGHT: This is the Model 10-67 oxygen mask, showing clearly the three straps and the leather fitting against the face. (Simon Lannoy Collection)

ABOVE: A LKp S100 helmet being worn with the three-strap 10-67 oxygen mask. (Mick Prodger Collection)

Section 3
GOGGLES

Pilots and crews in the Luftwaffe needed goggles for basic eye protection from dust rising up from the cockpit during combat, as well as to protect them from flying fragments of glass and perspex should their aircraft be hit. The problem that had to be overcome was that goggles had optical deficiencies, often causing loss of field of vision, reflection and they could also fog up at critical stages of the flight caused by hot breath and perspiration.

The fighter pilot with the best vision had the advantage over the enemy if they could pick out fighters at a distance. This would also require a good methodology of scanning the sky as it is a well-known issue in aviation that often you cannot pick out aircraft even at close range against a blue sky unless you move your head and scan the sky to pick up relative movement. Issues with badly-designed goggles would complicate matters and although the Luftwaffe sought to include all the ideal requirements into the development they eventually realised that it would be too much of a compromise to tick all the boxes.

However, the Luftwaffe goggles were of a much better design than those issued to the RAF as they realised that the larger they were the better the peripheral vision and that optical perfection was probably the highest on the desirability list. During the Battle of Britain period there were three principal types of goggles available. The most common were those that had a pair of large curved lenses held in metal frames which were in turn mounted on one-piece rubber eyepieces, although there was another type very similar with separate eyepieces. The third type were much smaller with oval lenses of tinted shatterproof glass which started off as sunglasses and developed into goggles. However, some pilots still went against orders and wore sunglasses in the cockpit.

WINDSCHUTZBRILLE MODEL 295 AND *FLIEGERSCHUTZBRILLE* MODEL 306

These goggles were manufactured by a number of different companies and came in two models, the model 295 and the 306. Both models of goggles have brass or aluminium frames which can be found painted in a variety of colours from a blue grey to field grey and even desert colour. They both have large optically-correct curved lenses in a teardrop shape. The goggles also enable enough room for wearing glasses underneath. These are secured to the helmet or head with an adjustable elasticated band. The Model 295 has a one-piece rubber face pad, often made by Auer, whereas the Model 306 has individual face pads for each of the lenses and also an adjustable bridge. There are variations in the design between manufacturers, such as on the adjustable bridge, where some have two screws to adjust rather than one. However, all models are stamped with a manufacturer's ID and a date of production.

ABOVE: The *Windschutzbrille* Model 295. These early goggles are dated 1935 and were worn throughout the war, originally for keeping dust out of the eyes and more for open cockpit/gunner type positions. The early ones came in an aluminium tin. They can be seen being worn in many Battle of Britain photos. (Mark Hillier Collection)

LEFT: The tin came with a small compartment which included spare lenses and also a spare strap, as well as the chin strap which could be fixed to the clips at the end of the eyepiece to hold the goggles in place in the strong slipstream. They were also produced without this additional clip. (Mark Hillier Collection)

ABOVE: The brass plate on the top of the tin shows the model and gives the date of manufacture amongst other information. This plate was later changed to aluminium. (Mark Hillier Collection)

RIGHT: Model 306 flying goggles with large curved lenses that provided an excellent field of vision. (Phil Phillips Collection)

THE LUFTWAFFE BATTLE OF BRITAIN FIGHTER PILOT'S KITBAG

SPLITTERSCHUTZBRILLE

The Luftwaffe had considered that preventing eye damage was an essential requirement of the goggles as flying shards of glass or Perspex could perforate the eye. The answer to the problem was the development of splinter proof goggles by Nitsche and Gunther. One common misconception with these is that it was thought they were shatterproof but in fact this is not the case

These were essentially round domed convex safety lenses which used Ultrasin glass which was very effective at reducing the sun's harmful rays and minimising refraction. These were particularly good at preventing small splinters in the eye.

They could be fitted with either clear or tinted lenses. The first issue was of a rigid construction with conventional arms just as sunglasses: the second attempt and more common was the pattern fitted with an elasticated head band, this was the more typical type seen in the Battle of Britain. The later types having a three-piece makeup for a more comfortable fit over the nose. These goggles were small enough to wear under the Model 295 or 306 if required.

LEFT: The single-piece second-pattern *Splitterschutzbrille* being worn on a summer LKp 100 flying helmet. Note the single piece bridge over the nose. (Paul Woodbyrne Collection)

GOGGLES

ABOVE LEFT: The single-piece second-pattern *Splitterschutzbrille* were supplied in a black tin which had the details of its contents stamped onto it. (Paul Woodbyrne Collection)

ABOVE RIGHT: The box and instructions for the single-piece second-pattern *Splitterschutzbrille*. (Phil Phillips Collection)

BELOW: Major Adolf Galland in his Bf 109E-4. Later, he had a telescopic gun sight fitted to his Bf 109E-4/N Wk Nr 5819. This photo shows him wearing the second-pattern *Splitterschutzbrille* goggles and what appears to be a net helmet. (Chris Goss)

ABOVE: A second-pattern pair of *Splitterschutzbrille* with an elastic strap. (Phil Phillips Collection)

SUNGLASSES

Although all of the goggles could be supplied with tinted lenses, the Luftwaffe pilots and crews also had available to them sunglasses which were popular. These included the Auer models S-100 and 101 fitted with tinted Neophan lenses. One rear gunner, Unteroffizier Max Guschewski, of 6/Zerstörergeschwader 76 was unfortunate to be hit by shrapnel which smashed his sunglasses in an

LEFT: These sunglasses are typical of the pre-war private purchase items that are often seen in many photos of Luftwaffe crews. The frames are tortoiseshell and the arms are a simple sprung wire that clips around the ear. The 'Made in Germany' marks were placed on German goods dating back as far as 1887 as part of the British introduction of the Merchandising Act. These sunglasses date to the 1930s and were for export but the Luftwaffe pilots wore them even though it was strictly against regulations to use them during flying. (Mark Hillier Collection)

action with Spitfires of 609 and 234 Squadrons over Salisbury, he no doubt chose the sunglasses over goggles as they offered better clarity when looking for enemy fighters: 'all of a sudden, I felt a fierce blow against my face – the thick rim of my sunglasses had been smashed by a shell splinter which then went into my left temple. Blood began to flow down my cheek and run over my life jacket. The same burst of fire blew out all the plexiglass panes in the cabin roof and the left engine was hit.' Their luck was to run out completely and despite a gallant effort to evade being shot down their Bf 110 eventually fell victim to its pursuers.³

RIGHT: This photo illustrates the reverse of the sunglasses, showing the leather shades to the sides of the arms. These too are marked 'Made in Germany'. Later in the war issue sunglasses were available. (Mark Hillier Collection)

RIGHT: Feldwebel Walter Meudtner of 3/Jagdgeschwader 51 in the cramped cockpit of his Bf 109E-1/E-3 in the early summer of 1940. He is wearing an LKp S 100 flying helmet and either sunglasses or first-pattern *Splitterschutzbrille* rather than flying goggles. He was killed in action on 26 September 1940. (Chris Goss)

Section 4
FLYING CLOTHING

It seems from surviving photos from the Battle of Britain period that the Luftwaffe pilots wore a wide variety of clothing, some choosing to fly in uniform or in shirtsleeves with a leather jacket over it, often with tight breeches or riding breeches with knee-length leather 'top' boots. Some just flew in uniform trousers and a jumper with no form of identification as described by Leutnant Erich Bodendieka, a Bf 109 pilot who was shot down and parachuted into captivity, landing in the sea off of Folkestone:

'I was collected by the Coastguards and overnight I was guest of the Royal Artillery in Folkestone. They were rather suspicious because I did not wear a normal uniform, only breeches and white socks (I had lost my fur-lined boots in the air) and a white pullover. I also had no identification, only my Iron Cross First Class which I had been awarded that afternoon.'[4]

Some did choose to wear the one-piece flying suits which were worn over the service uniform. There is a view that the fighter aircrew did not wear the one-piece suits but there are period photos showing Bf 110 and 109 pilots wearing the one-piece *Sommerfliegerkombi* (see below) so they are included in this publication. Some RAF pilots also chose to fly in one-piece suits but most were the lighter-weight privately-purchase type and generally not the Sidcot type.

The flying suits available as issue kit included a summer-weight flying overall and three winter-weight versions. The three winter variants have not been included in detail in this guide as they were generally worn by bomber crews and were too bulky for fighter cockpits, but photos have been included of the winter version and the Bavarian flight suit as they were available but not worn.

Although two-piece suits were available before the war, the fighter pilots did not really take to these until after the Battle of Britain. The other popular item, which was often a privately-purchased item, was the flight jerkin of which there were a number of styles. The Luftwaffe kit available for the Battle of Britain period was much the same as that available during the earlier Blitzkrieg periods and not much development of the equipment occurred until later on in the Second World War.

One thing that soon became apparent was that the pilots did not have much room to store equipment or places to carry it in their uniforms, particularly survival equipment and rations or more importantly first-aid kits in case of injury. Pockets were useful for items such as maps, chocolate, bandages, flares and gravity knives, amongst other desirables. Later on in the war, kit was specifically developed to house all of this equipment, and indeed the Luftwaffe were far in advance of the RAF in making kit for their pilots to suit their needs for survival on the ground or at sea, items such as the two-piece Channel Suit which came into service after the Battle of Britain, signal flags, one-man life rafts carried by the pilots etc.

FLYING CLOTHING

Very typical Battle of Britain Luftwaffe wear for operations by a Bf 110 rear gunner: early Hoffman of Berlin brown suede and leather boots with a single zip, *Sommerfliegerkombi* flying suit, back type parachute and 10-30 full back inflatable *Schwimmweste*. (Paul Woodbyrne Collection)

SOMMERFLIEGERKOMBI, SUMMER-WEIGHT FLYING COVERALL

This one-piece unlined flying suit is constructed from a heavy cotton fabric which has a brown and white flecked weave giving it a tan appearance. The suit features a long diagonal zip to allow ease of getting the item on. The cuffs are zipped with hidden elasticated inner cuffs. The fly has a

ABOVE: A briefing of Bf 110 crews of 3/Zerstörergeschwader 26, Conterville, September 1940. The figure in the centre is believed to be Hauptmann Gerhard Schoen. All are seen wearing the *Sommerfligerkombi* with the rank patches on the arm. The briefing is being conducted by Schoen over the bonnet of a captured British staff car. Two of the pilots in the centre are wearing the saddle form *Schirmmutze*, the one on the left the summer issue cap, and the NCO is wearing the *Fliegermutz* or side cap. All are wearing the 10-30 model *Schwimmweste* and a variety of silk scarves to prevent chaffing around the neck. (Chris Goss)

FLYING CLOTHING

RIGHT: This is the first pattern one-piece summer flight suit officially designated as *Fliegerschutzanzug fur Sommer* (*Kombination*) So/34. This flying suit was brought into service in 1934, made of a brown cotton fabric, and the first pattern can be distinguished by the horizontal fly. The suit was the mainstay for the Battle of Britain and can be seen in period photographs being often worn with a belt. It only remained in production until 1941 but was used throughout the war. (Phil Phillips Collection)

THE LUFTWAFFE BATTLE OF BRITAIN FIGHTER PILOT'S KITBAG

ABOVE: The label inside the suit shows the manufacturer and date of 1936, the unit markings stamped on it probably indicate Kampfgeschwader II Gruppe, Stukageschwader 165, a dive bomber unit. The Germans were very good at marking most items, even down to flying badges and awards, making them easier to identify. A later version of the flying suit carried a secondary emergency opening device to aid removal of clothing from injured aircrew. (Phil Phillips Collection)

horizontal zip, and there are map pockets provided to the chest with zipped pocket also on the legs for possible survival equipment. Rank insignia was normally worn on the arms between the elbow and the shoulder, normally being stitched onto a cloth of the same colour but the rank itself was in white for officers and NCOs, yellow for generals. This was worn with the leather belt. This was the most common flying coverall found being used by fighter aircrew.

OTHER FLYING COVERALLS

The Luftwaffe had available to them three other varieties of flying coverall although these were not widely used during the summer of 1940, although it may be that some aircrew opted for these when flying escort missions across the North Sea. They included the heavyweight fleece-lined flying suit for use during the winter months when flying over land: this was often referred to as a 'Bulgarian Suit', similar in design to the summer-weight type and a step-in item but again very heavy and bulky with a black fleece collar with the rank badges in a similar position to the summer suit. There was also a two-piece fleece-lined flying suit available for winter flights over the sea, normally made of brown

FLYING CLOTHING

RIGHT: An example of the KW33 one-piece winter flight suit, officially designated the *Fliegerschutzanzug fur Winter* (*Kombination*) *Baumuster* KW 1/33. Dating back to the 1930s it was designed for the open-cockpit aircraft of the period, very bulky and heavy, lined with a thick fleece. This particular example is not fitted with the concealed emergency aperture device of the later version. Photographs can be found of Bf 109 pilots wearing this in winter, pre-dating the Battle of Britain. One of the makers of this. and much of the flying clothing was Karl Heisler of Berlin. (Phil Phillips Collection)

THE LUFTWAFFE BATTLE OF BRITAIN FIGHTER PILOT'S KITBAG

LEFT: The all-leather Bavarian one-piece flying suit. Unlikely to have been worn by Battle of Britain Bf 109 and 110 crew, but as the Germans considered that the battle went on to April 1941, it is possible they were used by some in the winter months. (Phil Phillips Collection)

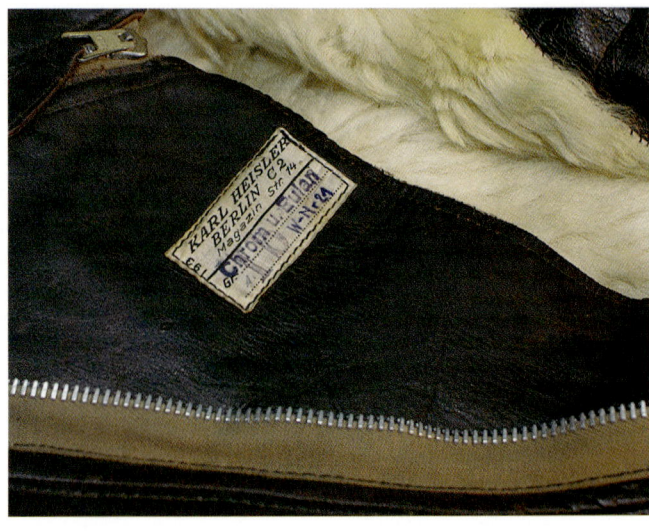

ABOVE: The manufacturer's label in the all-leather Bavarian one-piece flying suit. (Phil Phillips Collection)

FLYING CLOTHING

ABOVE: Leutnant Franz Fiby of 3/Jagdgeschwader 2 in a Bf 109E-3 coded Yellow 13. Note the Richthofen badge; the aircraft would have the blue 3/Jagdgeschwader 2 pennant on the cowling. Fiby survived the war. He is photographed here wearing a one-piece leather flying suit and the seat parachute has been left on the wing. (Chris Goss)

or black leather. The third was an electrically-heated flying suit which was worn over the normal uniform and under the outer flying suit which was plugged into the electrics of the aircraft: it was bulky and cumbersome and very unpopular. Mostly these were not regularly worn by fighter pilots during the Battle of Britain.

THE LUFTWAFFE BATTLE OF BRITAIN FIGHTER PILOT'S KITBAG

PRIVATE PURCHASE FLYING JACKETS

This was the most popular item of dress worn by the fighter crews as cockpit space was at a premium. These jackets were hard-wearing, warm and with zip-fastened pockets were much more practical. By 1940 although these had been sanctioned for wear it appears that they were mostly private purchases, many being of French manufacture, leading to a wide variety of styles and colours. Some squadrons, it is thought, ordered in bulk from certain manufacturers which is why in period photos it may appear that they are issue kit due to the uniformity, but this was not the case. Some jackets were modified to carry shoulder boards, extra loops for awards and other insignia. There are a wide range of types and colours seen from white to black leather, some with stitched woollen cuffs and some with just normal leather zipped cuffs, and others made from hard-wearing drill type material. All seem to have one thing in common in that they were tailored to the waist only. On the leather private purchase jackets the ranks were stitched onto shoulder boards.

ABOVE LEFT: An example of a private purchase leather jacket adapted for use by a pilot or aircrewman. The jacket has a cloth lining and cut to the waist, as were most jackets of this type. They offered warmth and practicality in the cockpit as they were close fitting. The eagle insignia can be seen over the left breast pocket. This was often in embroidered cloth, but pilots also chose to use the metal eagle from the summer uniform. All of the badges and awards were secured to the jacket by stitched loops so that they could easily be taken off without damaging the jacket. In this instance the shoulder board indicates the jacket belonged to a commissioned officer of the rank of Hauptmann. (Phil Phillips Collection)

ABOVE RIGHT: A close-up of the right-hand side of the jacket showing in better detail the breast eagle, rank boards and lining of the jacket. (Phil Phillips Collection)

FLYING CLOTHING

ABOVE: Oberleutnant Han-Karl Mayer, 1/Jagdgeschwader 53, killed in action on 17 October 1940. He is wearing a typical private purchase leather jacket and flyer's cap. (Chris Goss)

THE LUFTWAFFE BATTLE OF BRITAIN FIGHTER PILOT'S KITBAG

ABOVE: Bf 109s of 9/Jagdgeschwader 53 at Wiesbaden-Erbenheim, early 1940. Note that two of the Bf 109s have darkened camouflage on the rear fuselage and tail. The pilot in the centre is believed to be Leutnant Josef Volk. He wears a typical private purchase leather jacket of the period, and also has on the twin-zip model Pst 4004 flight boots, officers' flyer's cap and breeches. (Chris Goss)

LEFT: Major Werner Mölders of Jagdgeschwader 51 returns in his Bf 109 after a combat sortie over England. He looks exhausted and his ground crew are helping him take off his flying equipment and are about to hand him his service cap. Note he wears a private purchase leather jacket with fur-lined collar under his 10-30 life jacket. The shoulder boards for his rank have been sewn onto the jacket. (Mark Hillier)

FLYING CLOTHING

ABOVE: This front cover of an October 1940 edition of *Der Adler* carries a studio portrait of Major Werner Mölders. He is seen here holding his *Schirmmutze*, or uniform peaked cap, this one showing once again the typical 'saddle form' of the period; earlier models had a more saucer shape. Mölders is wearing his *Tuchrock*, or service tunic, with the silver officer's piping to the collar. Note the double-prong buckle on the brown leather belt for officers. He is wearing his Knight's Cross with Oak Leaves around his neck, this having been awarded in September 1940. The Flying Badge and Iron Cross First Class can be seen on his left breast pocket, whilst the button on his tunic carries the ribbon of the Iron Cross Second Class. Mölders' insignia indicate the rank of Major and would have the gold yellow *Waffenfarbe* of flying personnel. (Historic Military Press)

THE LUFTWAFFE BATTLE OF BRITAIN FIGHTER PILOT'S KITBAG

FLYING TROUSERS

Luftwaffe flying trousers with multiple pockets for housing survival equipment were available during 1940, These were not the established later variant known as 'Channel Trousers' but an earlier model made of dark grey velour with a crushed velvet lining similar to the electrically-heated suits. The waist is similar to the later issue 'Channel Trousers', with internal cinch belts and buckles inside the waist (belts are made of leather instead of webbing), buttons for suspenders/braces, rapid zip fly and two button top and zips at ankles. All zip fasteners are of metal. They had two large patch pockets on the front of the thighs for storing maps and equipment as well as two zip pockets (one on each outside leg) for survival equipment such as flares. Photographs exist of these trousers being worn during the Battle of Britain by Adolf Galland but were not widespread until the spring of 1941. The earliest known example dates back to the 1930s as shown in the photographs taken by Karl Heisler of Berlin.

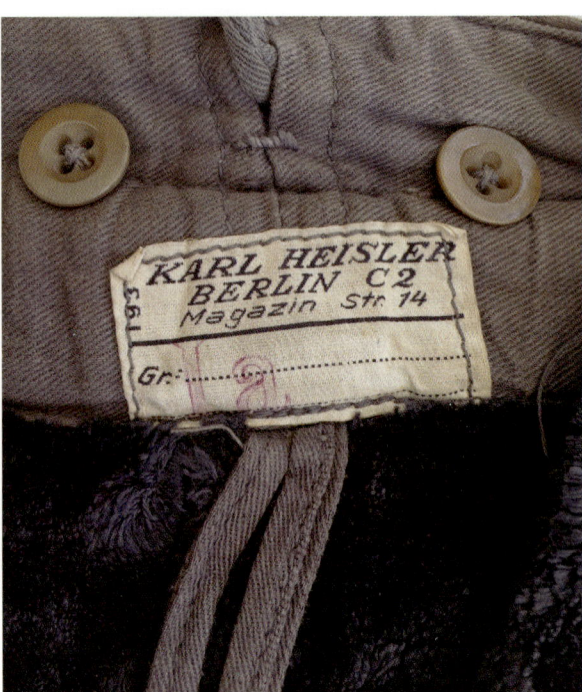

ABOVE and LEFT: A pair of early flying trousers dated as produced in the 1930s by Karl Heisler of Berlin. These early-style trousers feature two pouch pockets on the front of the legs for storage and two zipped side pockets on each leg with loops in them for flares. They are lined with a crushed velvet-type lining. Photographs exist of these trousers in use by Adolf Galland during the Battle of Britain, but they were not widespread until the spring of 1941. (Mark Hillier Collection)

FLYING CLOTHING

ABOVE: Seen by the tail of his Bf 109E-3 coded Black 1 is Hauptmann Horst Tietzen of 5/Jagdgeschwader 51. Tietzen's first kill after the Battle of France, his third overall, was a Blenheim on 27 June 1940. By the time this photo was taken he had shot down eighteen aircraft, the most recent being a Hurricane near Canterbury in the afternoon of 16 August 1940. He would get his twentieth just before his death in combat on 18 August 1940, his body being washed ashore later near Calais. He had shot down seven aircraft in Spain and would be posthumously awarded the Knight's Cross two days after his death. Here he can be seen wearing his 10-30 life-preserver but more interestingly is the blue-and-white polka dot scarf which was quite popular with fighter pilots. He also is wearing a private purchase leather jacket under his life jacket. (Chris Goss)

PILOTS' SCARVES

Just like the RAF had discovered, wearing a collar and tie in the cockpit often lead to great discomfort especially when turning your head rapidly from side to side to look for enemy aircraft. They too adopted silk scarves to help ease the chaffing, however they also served another purpose as illustrated by Gefreiter Josef Broeker, the pilot of a Bf 109 of 1/Jagdgeschwader 53 shot down on the 25 August 1940: ' I landed in a field and after I had regained my calmness, I set fire to my plane. I had put my silk scarf into the fuel injection pump and lit it with a match. The plane exploded and I suffered burns to my hand and face.'[5]

FLYING BOOTS

The Luftwaffe aircrews had available to them fleece-lined heavy-duty flying boots designed to be worn as part of the complete flying suit, but they are most often seen in period images with just the uniform. These were constructed of black leather around the foot area with the upper section being of soft black suede

ABOVE: At the start of the war, Oberleutnant Lothar Ehrlich was serving in 1/Jagdgeschwader 52. He is seen here on a Bf 109B/D when he was with 1/Jagdgeschwader 433 (named 1/Jagdgeschwader 52 from May 1939). In this photo he is wearing a summer flying suit and also the early PSt 3 brown leather and suede Hoffman boots. In March 1940, he moved to the recently formed 3/Jagdgeschwader 52 to command 8/Jagdgeschwader 52. He scored the Gruppe's first kill of the French campaign, a Curtiss Hawk south of Metz, on 18 May 1940. Having arrived on the Channel coast on 22 July 1940, on 24 July he, together with Major Wolf-Heinrich von Houwald (*Gruppen Kommandeur*), Oberleutnant Herbert Fermer (*Staffel Kapitän* 7/Jagdgeschwader 52) and Gefreiter Erich Frank (7/Jagdgeschwader 52), was shot down and killed over the Channel by Spitfires of 54 Squadron. Ehrlich's place was taken by Oberleutnant Günther Rall, who would become a highly successful fighter pilot with a distinguished post-war career. The following day, Fermer's replacement, Oberleutnant Wilhelm Keidel, and then his replacement, Oberleutnant Willy Bielefeld, were both shot down and killed over the Channel together with Leutnant Hans Schmidt, the *Gruppen Adjutant*. After such losses, 3/Jagdgeschwader 52 was withdrawn from the Channel Front on 1 August 1940, being redeployed to Zerbst for rest and refit. (Chris Goss)

which also had black leather reinforcing straps. They were zipped down both side for ease of access. Especially if the pilot was wounded or burned, the boots were easier to remove. They were secured to the leg by two leather straps and buckles. They were fleece-lined and nice and warm at altitude but they did have their drawbacks in that the fleece eventually wore down and this reduced their warmth over time, also they were not practical for walking in over long distances for aircrew who had been shot down.

Some pilots often chose to wear laced shoes or boots instead of the issue equipment. There is evidence that the same style of boot with only a single zip on one side was also available during the period. The single zip was introduced when it was realised that this version was just as easy to get on and off as the double zip, while also saving in the use of valuable materials.

The problem with flying in any boots is that they were not ideal if shot down and you landed in the Channel as described by Leutnant Karl-Joachim Eichhorn, 14 (Zerstörer)/Lehrgeschwader 1, a Bf 110 pilot: 'After touching the sea, the plane sank like a stone and I had some trouble in getting out. After some swimming and many trials (my flying boots were dragging me down), I finally succeeded in getting

ABOVE LEFT: These early brown leather and suede boots were manufactured by Hoffman of Berlin. These have just a single zip rather than the better-known two-zip black variant. The zip had a protective leather gusset to prevent it coming into contact with the wearer's skin. (Paul Woodbyrne Collection)

ABOVE RIGHT: Model Pst 4004 flight boots which were brought into service in 1937. The double-zip boots were made of leather on the lower area around the foot and suede uppers with leather straps. The inside was lined with lamb's wool. The idea of the double zip was that boots could be removed easily without causing further pain to a casualty. Eventually the wearing of riding boots and officers' boots was banned due to this reason late on in the Battle of Britain. The single-zip variety of the same pattern boot can also be seen being worn during the period. (Mark Hillier Collection)

THE LUFTWAFFE BATTLE OF BRITAIN FIGHTER PILOT'S KITBAG

into my dinghy'.[6] The idea of flying in riding boots, top boots etc. was frowned upon and against standing regulations as it made life difficult for groundcrews trying to help injured flyers when pulling the tight-fitting boots off, which could cause further pain and discomfort, especially for burns victims.

GLOVES

Leather gauntlet-style gloves which were sometimes fleece-lined and similar in style to the RAF issue were available along with a type with a shorter wrist. These are mainly found in black or brown leather. They were not popular with the fighter crews who preferred either private purchase thinner leather gloves or even knitted items which gave a better feel for flying the aircraft, the downside being less protection for the hands in a fire. Some of the Luftwaffe pilots even flew with their dress uniform gloves which were nice and thin to give a better feel.

LEFT: A selection of leather gauntlet gloves available to aircrew during the Battle of Britain, some with single-strap fasteners and some with double. All of these gloves are marked inside with the maker's details. Many pilots found these too cumbersome and opted to fly in service uniform gloves or private purchase short leather gloves. (Phil Phillips Collection)

FLYING CLOTHING

ABOVE LEFT and RIGHT: Examples of the stamps and makers' marks found inside the flight gauntlets. (Phil Phillips Collection)

RIGHT: Unteroffizier Karl Heinz Wilhelm of 3/Jagdgeschwader 7 stands in front of his Bf 109 somewhere in Germany, just before the Battle of Britain, wearing his flyer's blouse with long leather gauntlets on. He sports a pilot's badge which is pinned to his uniform through loops sewn on to the jacket. (Mark Hillier)

RIGHT: Some aircrew opted to use their service uniform gloves as shown here as they were supple kid leather or suede and offered a better feel on the controls than the leather gauntlets. (Phil Phillips Collection)

Section 5
LIFESAVING EQUIPMENT

Survival at sea after ditching an aircraft or parachuting into the water had a poor prognosis for all airmen during the Battle of Britain. Although the Luftwaffe had thought in depth about the purpose and design of their equipment, it seems that the life jacket was left wanting in a number of areas. Ideally you would want a jacket that would be tough enough to resist damage whilst in the cockpit and yet not restrict movement.

If used then you needed it to have sufficient buoyancy to keep an unconscious wearer afloat should they succumb to the cold, keep them floating the right way up, be visible, resistant to damage and keep on working for long enough to enable rescue. There were two types of life jacket available to the Luftwaffe in this period, one which was normally inflated with an inflation bottle. It was thought to have been favoured by the fighter pilots as it was not too bulky, but it had no inherent buoyancy unless it was inflated, although it could be topped up by mouth. The second type was the Kapok-filled life jacket which was bulky but did not require inflation to provide buoyancy. Unfortunately both models were not that satisfactory until modifications were made to them after lessons were learned during the Battle of Britain.

Often these jackets are seen with the pilot or crewman's signal mirror and wrist compass suspended from them, although during the Battle of Britain it was mainly only the compass. The Luftwaffe Bf 110s also carried inflatable dinghies which saved many crews. One unfortunate pilot who had to resort to the use of his dinghy was Hauptmann Hans Kogler, Staffel Kapitaen of 1/Zerstörergeschwader 26 who was shot down by Spitfires:

'The attack took place at about 1300 hrs and I ditched at about 1307–1310 hrs. I lost consciousness and when I awoke, found the cockpit full of water and so I had to get out before I was dragged down. My Bordfunker, Uffz Adolf Bauer, had managed to release the dinghy from the fuselage so we both swam and got in it. What followed was a hard time for both of us because we had nothing to eat and drink for the next four days. All such things as cake, water, chocolate and cigarettes were lost that night when the dinghy was capsized by a wave and it was not until the afternoon of Wednesday 14 August at about 1600 hrs that we were picked up by two E-boats in the vicinity of Nieuport.'[7]

The Bf 109 had a one-man dinghy behind the cockpit seat but the chance of getting this out after crashing in the Channel was remote. Later the Luftwaffe developed a one-man dinghy in a harness worn over the parachute but this is not included as it is thought to be post-Battle of Britain.

The Luftwaffe had thought a bit more about rescuing downed airmen and had set up the *Seenotdienst* as early as 1935. Although originally a civilian organisation, it was formally absorbed

LIFESAVING EQUIPMENT

into the Luftwaffe in July 1940. As the war loomed, the Luftwaffe procured a specific aircraft for the task in the Heinkel He 59 floatplane which were painted white with red crosses. These were soon targeted by the RAF after one aircraft was captured and it was seen that its pilot had taken notes on shipping movements, decreed to be military work.

The Air Ministry produced Bulletin 1254 approving these flying boats as legitimate targets, but sadly no doubt some that were destroyed may have been carrying RAF aircrew as much as Luftwaffe. These were equipped with long ladders to aid pick-up from the water and carried survival equipment. A number of floating buoys were placed in the Channel which were kitted out with rations etc., where aircrew could seek refuge and be picked up by rescue flying boats and E-boats. These buoys were the saviour, of many RAF crews as well. The Luftwaffe did carry basic survival aids, flare pistols and personal first-aid dressings, more than their counterparts, the RAF not even having a life raft at this stage of the war for the fighter pilots.

SCHWIMMWESTE, THE INFLATABLE LIFE JACKETS

It was thought that this style of jacket was popular with the fighter pilots as it was normally deflated and very lightweight although it's clear from period photos that both types were worn by all crews. It was of a waistcoat style, made of rubberized canvas and had an inflatable bladder around the front and around the back which was inflated by a CO_2 cartridge, the cylinder for which was attached to the front lower left hand side of the jacket. The jacket could also be filled or topped up by using the oral inflation tube which was fitted with a one way valve vertically up the front of the jacket.

RIGHT: The front of the waistcoat-style life preserver, the Model SWp734, which was developed by Drager in the late 1930s. This example was made at the Dragerwerk factory in Lübeck on 6 July 1939. It was manufactured in yellow rubberized canvas with a single continuous inflatable chamber. Three simple canvas straps with ring buckles fasten at the front and a single strap passed between the legs. A carbon dioxide cylinder was provided for inflation; this was situated on the lower left lobe and operated via a screw valve. A rubber oral inflation tube was provided so the wearer could 'top-up' the pressure if necessary. This early pattern, designated as a Model SWp734 on the label, pre-dated the 10-30 and has a 'full back'. It has the early metal screw valve on the CO_2 cylinder although fitted with a later plastic mouthpiece – perhaps as a result of damage to the original metal one. (David Farnsworth Collection; www.historicflyingclothing.com)

ABOVE: The Model 10-30 inflatable life-preserver made of rubberized canvas was developed by Dräger back in 1936–7. It is secured by canvas straps across the front and another up between the legs. It is inflated by an oxygen bottle and can be toped up by a mouth tube. This one dates to August 1940 and is marked internally '26' in red which could relate to Jagdgeschwader 26. It was originally thought that these were the preserve of the fighter pilots but actually photos can be found of fighter crews wearing both the 10-30 and the Kapok versions. This model has a full back panel which could, if the pilot was unconscious, lead to them floating face down and drowning, It was later modified to an open back and securing straps. (Mark Hillier Collection)

LIFESAVING EQUIPMENT

ABOVE and RIGHT: The rear of the waistcoat-style life preserver, the Model 10-30. It was manufactured in yellow rubberized canvas with a single continuous inflatable chamber. Three simple canvas straps with ring buckles fasten at the front and a single strap passed between the legs. A carbon dioxide cylinder was provided for inflation; this was situated on the lower left lobe and operated via a screw valve. (Mark Hillier Collection)

THE LUFTWAFFE BATTLE OF BRITAIN FIGHTER PILOT'S KITBAG

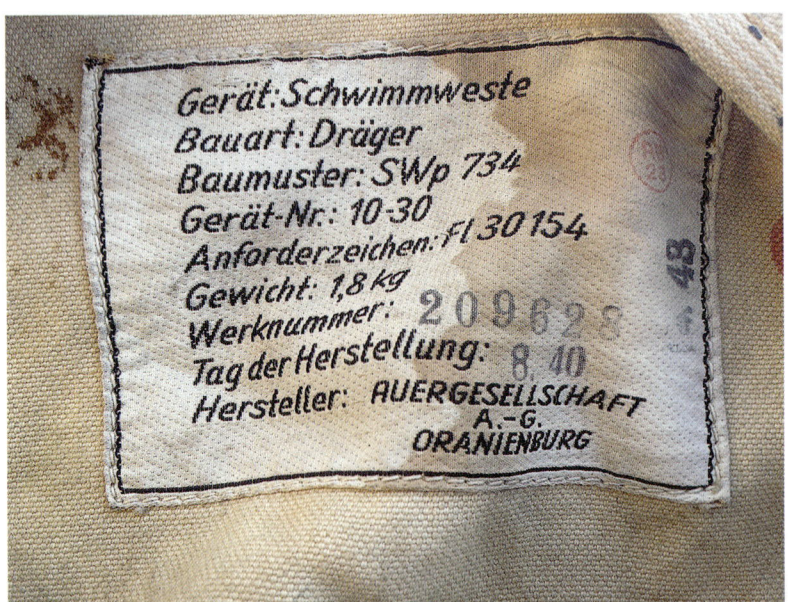

LEFT: The label of the Model 10-30 shows it as having been manufactured by Drager in August 1940. (Mark Hillier Collection)

LIFESAVING EQUIPMENT

ABOVE: A group of pilots of 3/Jagdgeschwader 53, Le Touquet, October 1940 getting ready to fly wearing mostly *Fliegerbluse* and life jackets. The NCO on the far left is wearing a 10-30 B2 life-preserver with a single strap at the back and less buoyancy than the earlier 10-30 model to ensure the pilot floated face up in the water if unconscious. The pilot with his back to the camera wears a Kapok life jacket. All are wearing the twin zip black leather and suede flying boots. (Chris Goss)

OPPOSITE BELOW: Personnel from the highly successful Stab 3/Jagdgeschwader 51 seen at St Omer/Clairmarais in the summer of 1940, all wearing the Model 10-30 inflatable life preserver with the full back and flyer's cap for officers. The officer on the far right has a dye pack hanging from his life-preserver. They are, left to right, Oberleutnant Otto Kath (Adjutant), Leutnant Werner Pichon-Kalau (*Technischer Offizier*) wearing his service uniform or *Tuchrock*, Leutnant Herbert Wehnelt (*Nachrichten Offizier*), and Hauptmann Hannes Trautloft (*Gruppen Kommandeur*). Trautloft would take command of Jagdgeschwader 54 on 24 August 1940 and end the Battle of Britain with eight kills. Kath (who moved with Trautloft to Jagdgeschwader 54) would shoot down two, as would Wehnelt. Pichon-Kalu would also accompany Trautloft to Jagdgeschwader 54, shooting down six by the end of the Battle of Britain. All four survived the war. (Chris Goss)

The jacket was secured to the wearer by three buckled straps down the side of it. One drawback was that it only had a single chamber and was susceptible to damage. Also it provided as much buoyancy at the rear as at the front which would possibly drown an unconscious airmen. It was manufactured in several colours from Luftwaffe blue grey to brown, but most from the Battle of Britain period seem to be a red or pale yellow colour to help facilitate air-sea rescue. However, the early issue type with the full back on the waistcoat had some drawbacks, in particular that it made the pilot sweat heavily. The B model of the same jacket that was available during the latter part of the Battle of Britain had a reduced cut to the rear of the waistcoat which helped with keeping the wearer's head out of the water.

ABOVE: The *Schwimmweste* being worn over the officer's *Tuchrock* of an Oberleutnant. In the early part of the battle fighter pilots often would just fly in their service uniform with life jacket over it, riding breeches and top boots or long trousers and shoes. (Mark Hillier Collection)

LIFESAVING EQUIPMENT

KAPOK-FILLED LIFE JACKET MODEL 10-76A

The Kapok jacket was a much bulkier garment, again in the form of a waistcoat, with floatation front and back. The Kapok was in tight rolls vertically up the front and back of the jacket, tied every 6in, making the rolls look like sausages. The life jacket was secured at the front with wooden pegs.

RIGHT: A full back Kapok *Schwimmweste* model 10-76A which was worn by both fighter and bomber crews. This full back type was later changed to having no back and only securing straps as too much buoyancy was provided on the early type, which meant that unconscious aircrew could end up floating face down in the water. (Paul Woodbyrne Collection)

55

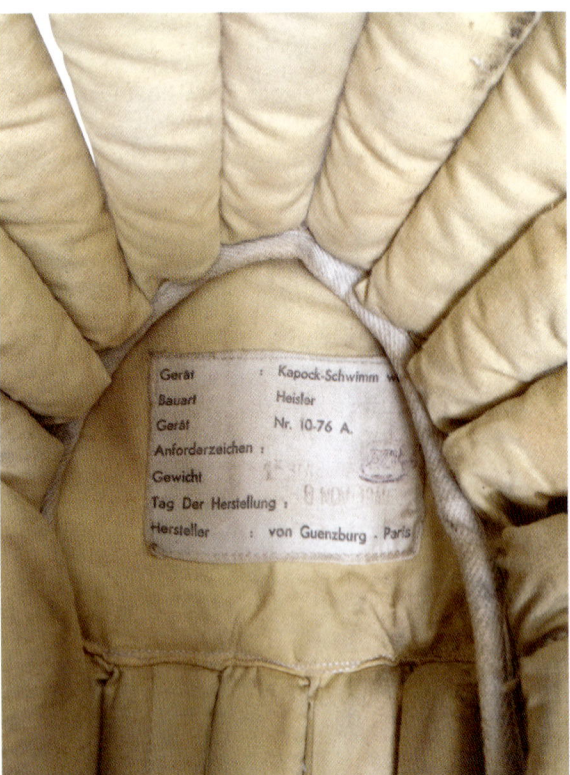

LEFT: The label inside this example shows it was manufactured in November 1940.

RIGHT: An unidentified pilot from what is believed to be Jagdgeschwader 2, probably celebrating his return after a successful mission. He is wearing the bulky 10-76A Kapok-filled life-preserver and what appears to be a pair of first pattern *Nitsche und Günther Splitterschutzbrille* (anti-splinter) glasses. Also note the marker dye bag attached to the front of the life jacket at bottom right. (Chris Goss)

LIFESAVING EQUIPMENT

As long as the jacket was in good condition it would keep the wearer afloat for about 24 hours. There were two distinct problems with the jacket, however, one being that although it had a stand-up collar to help keep the wearer's head above water, since there was more Kapok in the back, the poor airman could end up floating face down in the water. The other issue was that the Kapok, designed to absorb water as part of its buoyancy, would also absorb aviation fuel and oil into it and if it caught light it could turn the poor aircrew into a human torch. Later models had less buoyancy at the back, keeping the aircrew floating face-up.

SEAT-TYPE PARACHUTE '*SITZFALLSCHIRM*' (FI 30231)

The Bf 109 was principally designed with a bucket-type seat that enabled the pilot to wear a seat-type parachute. To look at, it is very similar in design to those used by the RAF due to the fact that the Germans had purchased harnesses from the British Irvin company before the war and the design of the buckles, quick release etc. were of superior design to those in use at the time in Germany so they copied the concept. It fastened across the chest with a central quick-release box and D-type pull ring mounted on the left-hand side.

Aircrew practised the sequence of abandoning the aircraft time and time again. The Bf 109 had a side hinged canopy which meant that it had to be jettisoned to get out as opening it normally would have been virtually impossible with the slipstream and also imagine the G forces working against the pilot who could experiencing very high G in an aircraft out of control. Ulrich Steinhilper wrote about jettisoning the canopy after being hit by a stray flak shell in his Bf 109 over France and his aircraft fell out of control, 'There was no more time to think now; I would have to get out whilst I could. Hurry! I pulled the emergency lever and the canopy rumbled down the fuselage. Get out! Get out! Radio jack plug out. Release harness and push up.'[8] He successfully made it out and his parachute deployed.

However, many pilots died as a result of this design, due to the problems caused during landing accidents and nose-overs or fires where opening the cockpit canopy was a problem, The aircraft would need to be lifted up to be able to open the canopy back on the hinge. Why choose this design? It was, of course, quicker and easier to manufacture. Once the hood had been dealt with, as long as the aircraft was structurally complete, pilots had a few moments to think and then act.

The sequence of bailing out is described nicely by Leutnant Albert Striberny, of 3/Lehrgeschwader 2 who was in action against 54 Squadron Spitfires on 8 July 1940: 'I heard the sound as if one throws peas against a metal sheet and my cabin was full of dark smoke. I felt splashes of fuel on my face so I switched off the electrical system, dived back into cloud and threw off the cabin roof. The smoke disappeared and I could breathe freely and noticed from the wings there came white streams of glycol. Whilst diving I tried several times to start the engine, switching on the electrical system, but in vain. When I came out of cloud, I decided to bale out and undid the clasp of my seat belt and was about to climb onto the seat and jump when I thought about the speed of the aircraft and I was afraid to be thrown against the tail plane so I pulled back the stick and slowed the aircraft down. This took a matter of seconds; I did have a half roll and fell out. As I was a bit afraid to mix up the handle for opening the parachute and the press button that holds the parachute straps, I put my right hand on the handle and rolled the aircraft with the left. When falling, I didn't notice very much but, as we were told, counted to twenty-three then pulled the handle and after the drogue had opened over me, I felt a sudden jerk and hung under the opened parachute.'[9]

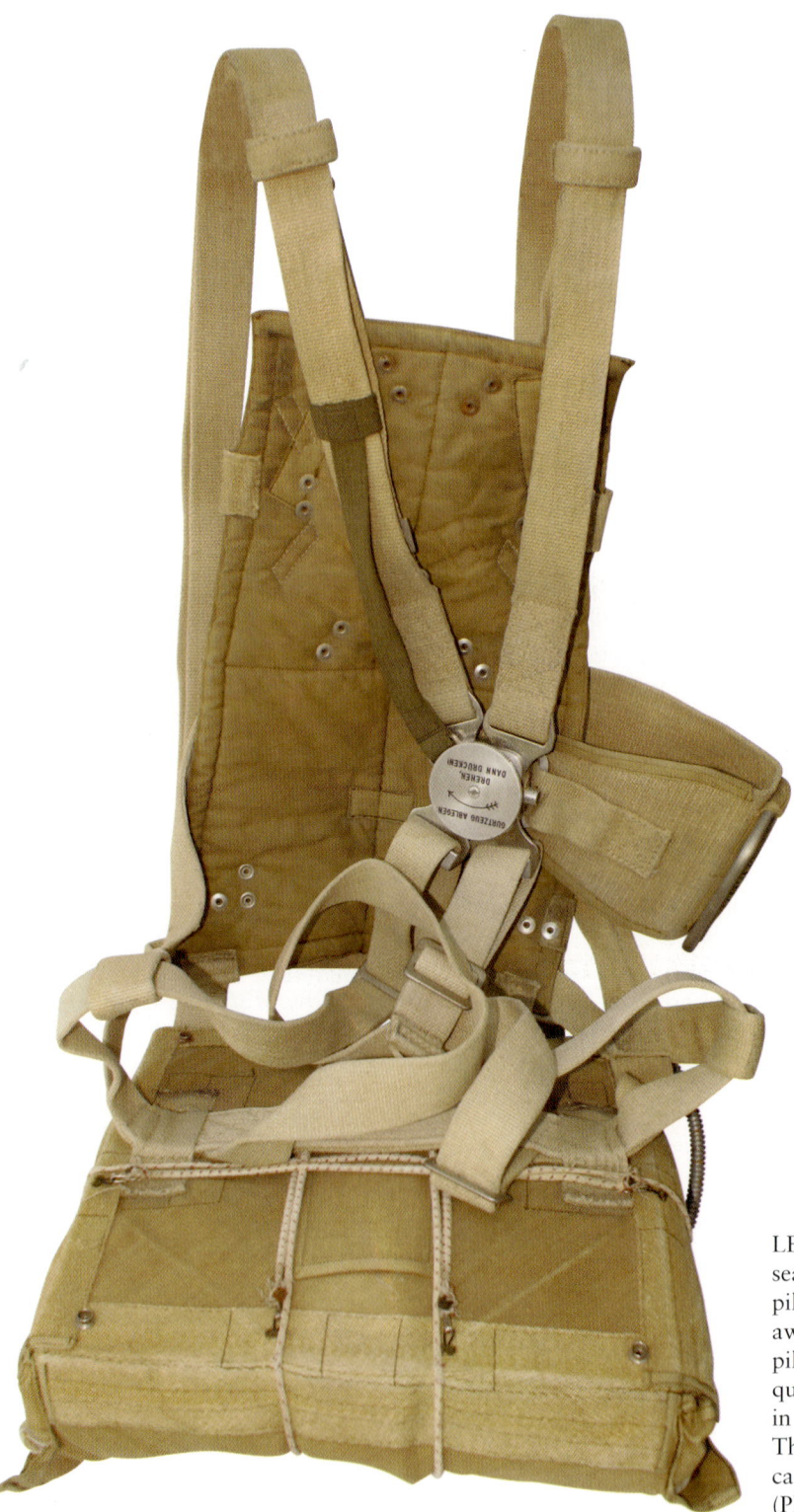

LEFT: A '*Sitzfallschirm*' (FI 30231) seat-type parachute used by fighter pilots. The parachute is packed away in the seat part which the pilot sits on. The harness and quick-release box are very similar in style to RAF types of the period. The D ring to deploy the parachute can be seen on the right-hand side. (Phil Phillips Collection)

LIFESAVING EQUIPMENT

But the margin for error was very small and the fine line between a successful bailout and certain death is evident in accounts such as that by Oberleutnant Anton Stangle, an ace of 5/Jagdgeschwader 54 who had collided with another Bf 109 in a dogfight over Kent on 1 September 1940. He had lost part of his wing in a collision and had only seconds to react before the aircraft went into an uncontrollable spin into terra firma or the Channel.

'We were ordered to escort a Kampfgruppe which was attacking the harbour facilities east of London. We soon had contact with British Fighters and my Staffel had been split up and each Rotte was having to fight by themselves. I noticed a Spitfire about 800m below me and I knew

RIGHT: A close-up shot of the quick-release mechanism on the seat-type parachute. (Phil Phillips Collection)

THE LUFTWAFFE BATTLE OF BRITAIN FIGHTER PILOT'S KITBAG

ABOVE: A Bf 109E-1 coded Red 7 of 2/Jagdgeschwader 20. This photograph was probably taken at Brandenburg-Briest between September and November 1939. At the time 2 Staffel was commanded by Oberleutnant Albrecht 'Minni' Freiherr von Minnigerode; the unit was re-designated 8/Jagdgeschwader 51 in July 1940. Note the Black Cat emblem of 2/Jagdgeschwader 20 on the cowling. The pilot is wearing a seat-type parachute of the kind mainly used by Bf 109 pilots during the Battle of Britain. He is also wearing the summer flying suit. (Chris Goss)

immediately that I had an excellent chance of shooting him down so I called up my Rottenflieger and told him to be ready to roll over and attack. Now I did what I always did before rolling over – I started looking back to the left and saw another Bf 109 of an unknown unit some fifty or sixty metres away with its airscrew shining in the sun approaching me at full speed. That look behind saved my life. I realised immediately that a collision was unavoidable, so I pushed my control column forwards and to the right and felt a tremendous shock of the crash. My head was thrown forwards and hit the gunsight and I blacked out. A few seconds later, I came to and saw that my left wing had gone and a white fountain was shooting out of the engine cowling just a metre in front of me. Now I reacted as I had been taught at least a hundred times during training. Waiting and thinking for a moment, throwing off the canopy and bailing out. I was thrown out with terrible force and hit my left foot on the part of the canopy which was not jettisoned. I now fell through the air – a wonderful experience – and after waiting, opened my parachute. It opened at once at about 19,000ft and it took me half an hour to come down. The view was

LIFESAVING EQUIPMENT

ABOVE: This pilot of Zerstörergeschwader 26, equipped with the Bf 110, has a helping hand to get him up onto the wing of his aircraft. He is wearing a summer flying suit, and flying boots as well as a 10-30 life jacket. He also has on a seat-type parachute whereas the rear crewman would wear the back type. The German press photo carries a date on the reverse of August 1940. The pilot is wearing what appears to be a net helmet. (Mark Hillier)

excellent – I could see much of the English Channel, Dungeness on one side, on the other, Calais and the woods some kilometres to the east where our improvised airfield lay.'[10]

BACK TYPE PARACHUTE – *RÜCKENFALLSCHIRM* (Fl 30245)

Typically this type of parachute was worn by crews who had a recess in the seat back accommodating the parachute rather than the seat pan, depending on the aircraft type. It differed considerably in that the rear compact parachute back was fitted into an aluminium tray. The harness was similar to that of other types, as was the quick-release mechanism. The early version of this was closed up with interlocking teeth from which the wearer had to pull out the locking pin to deploy the chute.

THE LUFTWAFFE BATTLE OF BRITAIN FIGHTER PILOT'S KITBAG

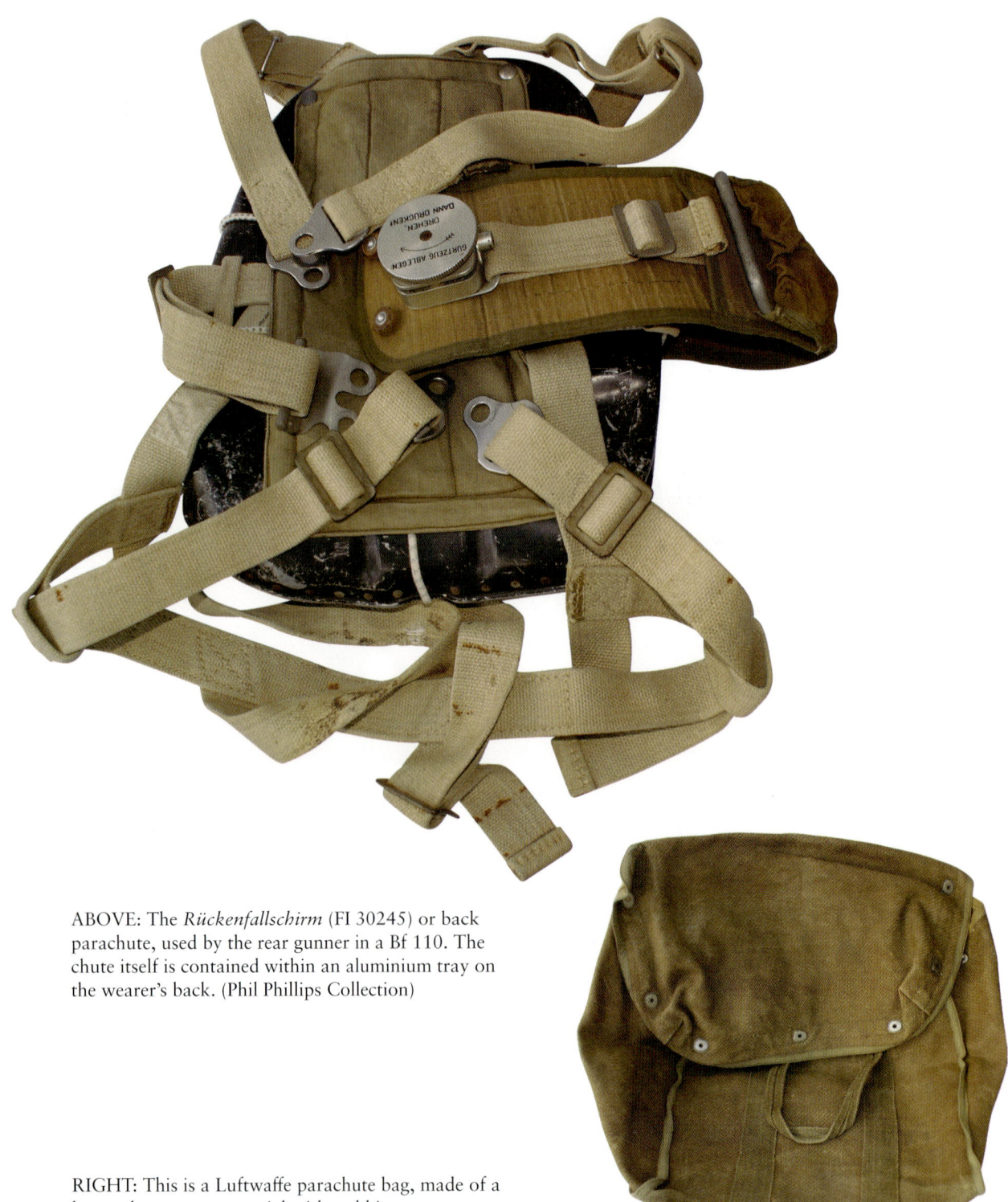

ABOVE: The *Rückenfallschirm* (Fl 30245) or back parachute, used by the rear gunner in a Bf 110. The chute itself is contained within an aluminium tray on the wearer's back. (Phil Phillips Collection)

RIGHT: This is a Luftwaffe parachute bag, made of a heavy-duty weave material with webbing carry straps stitched to it. (Phil Phillips Collection)

LIFESAVING EQUIPMENT

LUFTWAFFE *EINMANNSCHLAUCHBOOT* FOR THE BF 109 AND THE LATER *PACKHULLE* FOR WEAR WITH THE SEAT-TYPE PARACHUTE

Although not personal issue during the Battle of Britain, it is worth mentioning the situation with regards survival at sea for the Luftwaffe fighter crews as they were much better prepared than their RAF counterparts. The Luftwaffe developed a fighter pilot's one-man raft and this was fitted behind the seat in the Bf 109 with paddles during the Battle of Britain period. Unfortunately, however, it was very difficult to deploy after a crash into the Channel. Even if the aircraft did come down at a shallow angle onto a calm sea it would still disappear beneath the waves with alarming rapidity.

Adolf Galland, the commander of Jagdgeschwader 26, commented on the preference of his pilots to ditch rather than parachute out over the Channel in order to get their life raft out and delay the inevitable onset of hypothermia. A nice ideal but easier said than done, as many were to find out to their cost. Galland stated:

'It turned out that a forced landing on the water was preferable to a parachute descent into the sea [maybe due to the fact that rumours were rife of pilots machine-gunning aircrew in their parachutes]. After touch down on the water, the plane remained afloat between 40–60 seconds, just about long enough for the pilot to unstrap himself and scramble out. The lucky ones were fished out of the water by the tireless Air Sea Rescue Service. Mae West, rubber dinghy, coloured flare bag, Very pistol and other useful trifles may have weighed the pilot down like Father Christmas, but they turned out to be excellent accessories.'[11]

Later, and it is thought after the Battle of Britain, a sling-type pack with a one-man dinghy in it was developed for wear at the discretion of the pilot. The pack containing the raft was constructed of green canvas and was a rectangular in shape with crossed shoulder straps clipped around the waist and was worn under the parachute harness like a waistcoat. The dinghy, normally a Type A-1, had a CO_2 inflation cylinder.

The Bf 110 also had a larger two-man dinghy which was equipped with rations and supplies, again fitted in the fuselage but these were not personal issue so have not been included.

FLARE PISTOL

Most of the single-seat fighter pilots carried a standard single-barrel flare pistol (*Leuchtpistol*) which had a simple break-open action in which a single flare cartridge would be inserted. A variety of cartridges with various colour stars and numbers of stars would be carried, ideal for attracting the attention of passing E-boats or flying boats. Even in the summer, the temperature of the water and the tides were a constant threat to the downed aircrew: the quicker they could bring attention to themselves, the greater the chance of survival. Also the chance of spotting a person in the sea from above is very slim.

Many pilots also tried to use their flare pistol to set fire to their aircraft after a forced landing to stop the enemy getting any intelligence or technology, as described by Oberleutnant Victor Mölders, a Bf 109 pilot of 2/Jagdgeschwader 51: 'I eventually had to crash land on top of an anti-tank ditch and did so too successfully – the aircraft showed no signs of burning. I tried to get out the flare pistol but couldn't and setting my map alight with my lighter and trying to start a fire also failed to destroy my aircraft'[12] Larger aircraft, such as the Bf 110 or He 111, would carry a double-barrelled flare pistol.

THE LUFTWAFFE BATTLE OF BRITAIN FIGHTER PILOT'S KITBAG

ABOVE LEFT and RIGHT: These photos show a very typical example of the flare pistol carried by the Luftwaffe in the Battle of Britain. This one is dated 1940 and manufactured by Erma Erfurt. Although the serial number of this one indicates it was most likely in police use, the pattern is the same. To break open the pistol there is a catch on the front of the trigger guard. These pistols had a ring on the grip for attaching a lanyard. (Mark Hillier Collection)

ABOVE: A Walther Heeres-Modell flare pistol. This is the later aluminium alloy version which was produced from 1934 onwards. This actual example was recovered from the wreckage of Dornier Do.17/Z-2 coded 5K+AR, with the *werke nummer* 1160 and operated by 7/III KG3, which was forced down by Boulton Paul Defiants of 264 Squadron on 26 August 1940. The wreckage was recovered from the Goodwin Sands in 2013, at which point this flare pistol, seen here after completion of conservation work, was found in the cockpit. Although in this instance from a bomber crew, this type of flare pistol was carried by fighter pilots in the Battle of Britain. (Historic Military Press)

LIFESAVING EQUIPMENT

LEFT: An example of early leg straps to hold flares. During the Battle of Britain period these would have been locally made by the groundcrew or aircrew and they are mainly scraps of webbing and buckles taken from other items of kit. Later in the war an issue flare leg strap was available. Also shown is the variety of colours of flare cartridges that were carried. The round Bakelite box is an example of a flare container. Flares were not just for air-sea rescue purposes but also for recognition signals. (Phil Phillips Collection)

RIGHT: A further example of early leg straps to hold flares. (Paul Woodbyrne Collection)

LUFTWAFFE FIGHTER PILOT'S LEG/BOOT FLARE STRAP

The issue variety commonly seen was post-Battle of Britain and made of blue-grey cloth for carrying up to ten flare cartridges in loops, 24.5in long x 1.5in wide, worn by Luftwaffe crews around the lower leg above or sometimes over the top of the flying boot. The blue-grey cotton fabric is marked with the RB number 0/1001/10038. What is clear from surviving photos and examples is that pilots had similar items made up on station to carry the flares before the issue type, made of webbing straps, elastic loops and buckles. There is an account by Oberleutnant Hans Theodor Grisebach of 2/Jagdgeschwader 2 that confirms he had flares strapped to the top of his flying boots: 'It was a lovely summer's day when we took off on an escort mission over Portsmouth. It was so warm, all I was wearing was a shirt, blue trousers, flying boots with flares strapped to the top, a flying helmet and life jacket. I also carried a pistol.'[13]

ABOVE: Hauptmann Wilhelm Balthasar preparing for a mission. His Bf 109E-4 carried the 3/Jagdgeschwader 3 axe on the yellow cowling whilst it also carried 1/Jagdgeschwader 1's Jesau cross (carried also on 3/Jagdgeschwader 27 aircraft) below the cockpit. He is flying in his *Fliegerbluse* with a 10-30 *Schwimmweste*. His ground crew behind are helping him with his seat-type parachute. The other ground crew member is filling up his flare bandolier around the top of his black leather and suede twin-zip flying boots. He wears a pair of short leather gloves, probably private purchase. On his right side appears to be a dye pack hanging down from the *Schwimmweste*. (Chris Goss)

LIFESAVING EQUIPMENT

ABOVE and RIGHT: This is a gravity knife of the type carried by Luftwaffe aircrew during the Battle of Britain. It has a concealed blade which can be released by pushing a spring lever whilst pointing the knife downwards and then locked in place. These were often secured to pockets by a lanyard. The later type had a modification in that it could be taken apart to replace the blade and spring. (Phil Phillips Collection)

GRAVITY KNIFE

All aircrew were issued with a knife which had a retractable blade to assist in ditching or for survival purposes, the knife was secured by a lanyard that could be secured to a loop in the early-style 'Channel trousers' or flying suit. The concealed blade was released by pressing a spring lever while pointing the knife downwards and the blade then locked into place. This was known as the first pattern which had no means of disassembly and if the spring broke inside the knife was then useless. A second pattern, the 'take down version', became available it is thought in 1941 which could be dissembled and repaired.

THE LUFTWAFFE BATTLE OF BRITAIN FIGHTER PILOT'S KITBAG

LUFTWAFFE PILOT AND NAVIGATOR'S (OBSERVER'S) *ARMBANDKOMPASS* AK39

The Luftwaffe issued every aircrew member the *Armbandkompass* which had a large oversized leather strap so that it could be worn over the flying clothing or in some photos it can be seen tied onto the *Schwimmweste* or looped around the waist belt. The early pattern compass had a black face with white numbers depicting the degrees. The main reason for issue of this was not for aircraft navigation but for use as a survival aid.

LEFT: An early AK39 *Armbandkompass* (first model variation) with a black dial and white numbers with a solid back which only had the manufacturing and compass details on it. This type is typical of the period and seen in many Battle of Britain Luftwaffe photos. (Mark Hillier Collection)

BELOW: This is a later AK39 model number 23235-1 in its box which is dated 2 December 1940. The later variant was easier to read at night and also had sighting lines on the top of the face. (Phil Phillips Collection)

LIFESAVING EQUIPMENT

ABOVE: Oberfeldwebel Magnus 'Ghandi' Brunkhorst, 9/Jagdgeschwader 2. His first kill was a Spitfire off the Isle of Wight in the afternoon of 18 August 1940. This photo was taken on 6 November 1941 after he had just shot down a Whirlwind of 263 Squadron, but his equipment is typical of the Battle of Britain period. He wears a private purchase leather jacket with a 10-30 life jacket, upon which he wears an AK39 wrist compass. (Chris Goss)

LUFTWAFFE SIGNAL MIRROR 'BLENDSPIEGEL'

Polished steel reflective 'mirror' measuring 6.25in x 3.25in (160mm x 83mm) which normally had an instruction decal on the 'non-polished' side. These came with a soft cotton-fitted slip case, either white or yellow, printed with '*Blendspiegel*' and FL 415610. Carried by Luftwaffe aircrews, mainly fighter pilots, in the pocket of their flight suits or 'Channel trousers' and used in the event of crashing, ditching or baling out to attract the attention of aircraft and ships while awaiting rescue. The exact date of introduction is not known but it is certainly thought to have been available in early 1941 if not before.

THE LUFTWAFFE BATTLE OF BRITAIN FIGHTER PILOT'S KITBAG

LEFT and BELOW: A Luftwaffe signal mirror in a marked white canvas case, often secured to the individual with a lanyard to a pocket but some pilots chose to fix them onto their life jacket. If you were shot down over the sea this could be used for signalling to a passing aircraft or ship by reflecting the sun's rays. These could be seen for some considerable distance but again only in line of sight, and it would be very difficult to signal ships in a heavy swell. (Mick Prodger Collection)

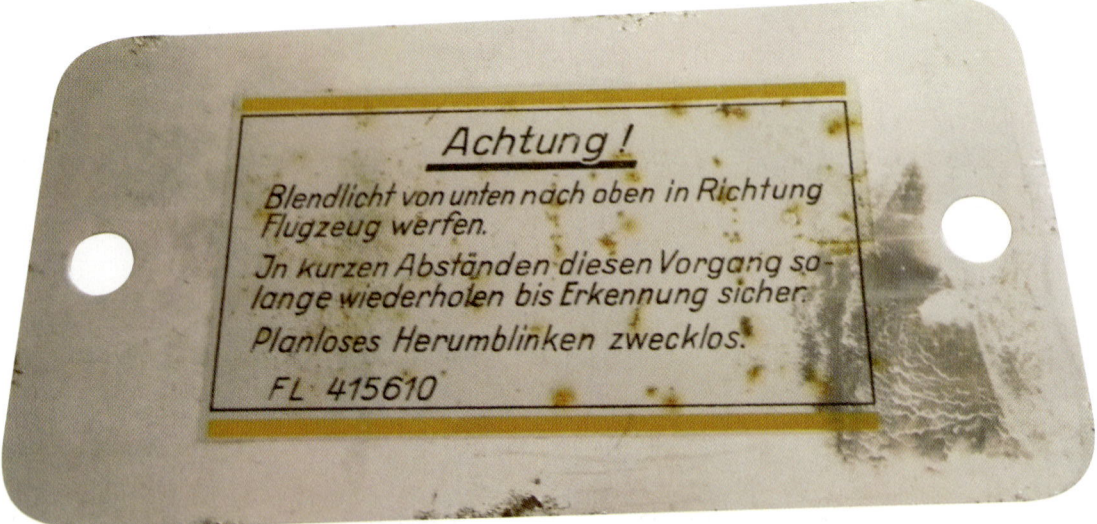

LUFTWAFFE DYE PACK OR *FARBBEUTEL* ('BAG OF COLOURS')

The idea was that this bag of marker dye would be carried by the pilot for use after ditching. When an aircraft came into sight the pilot would pour the dye into the sea and the surrounding colour change would attract the attention of the search vessel or aircraft. You would not want to deploy the marker dye on landing in the water as often the raft or aircrew in a life jacket would drift away from the patch of sea that had been stained. Used correctly at the right time, it greatly increased the chance of being spotted by passing aircraft.

Feldwebel Heinrich Hoehnisch, a Bf 109 pilot, gives testimony to the use of the dye pack when he witnessed the demise of a damaged Bf 109 of his squadron on return from operations during the Battle of Britain: 'The French coast was visible in the haze but he was too low. His plane's shadow on the water came nearer and nearer and a fountain of spray appeared in the sea and the Messerschmitt could no longer be seen. Suddenly the tail broke to the surface and I saw Ruehl in the water. Immediately, the water around him was coloured yellow. I flew around the spot to make sure he was still alive and then headed for France.'[14]

LIFESAVING EQUIPMENT

ABOVE: A further variant of a pilot's dye bag. (Mick Prodger Collection)

LEFT: A first-pattern Luftwaffe dye pack or *Farbbeutel* ('Bag of Colours'). There are first-hand accounts of this being used during the Battle of Britain to aid being spotted when in the sea. These are now extremely rare and hard to find. (Mick Prodger Collection)

WOUND DRESSINGS AND FIRST AID KITS

There is evidence that most pilots and crews carried wound dressings in sterile packs win their trousers but first-hand accounts show also that some took personal first aid kits with them as described by Oberleutnant Rudolf Moellerfriedrich, a Bf 109 pilot of 6/Jagdgeschwader 2, who was shot down on 18 August 1940: 'My parachute opened successfully and I proceeded to bandage my arm and hand with the first aid kit in my pocket.'[15] First aid kits were often found in larger aircraft but in 1941 smaller first aid kits suitable for single-seat fighters became available.

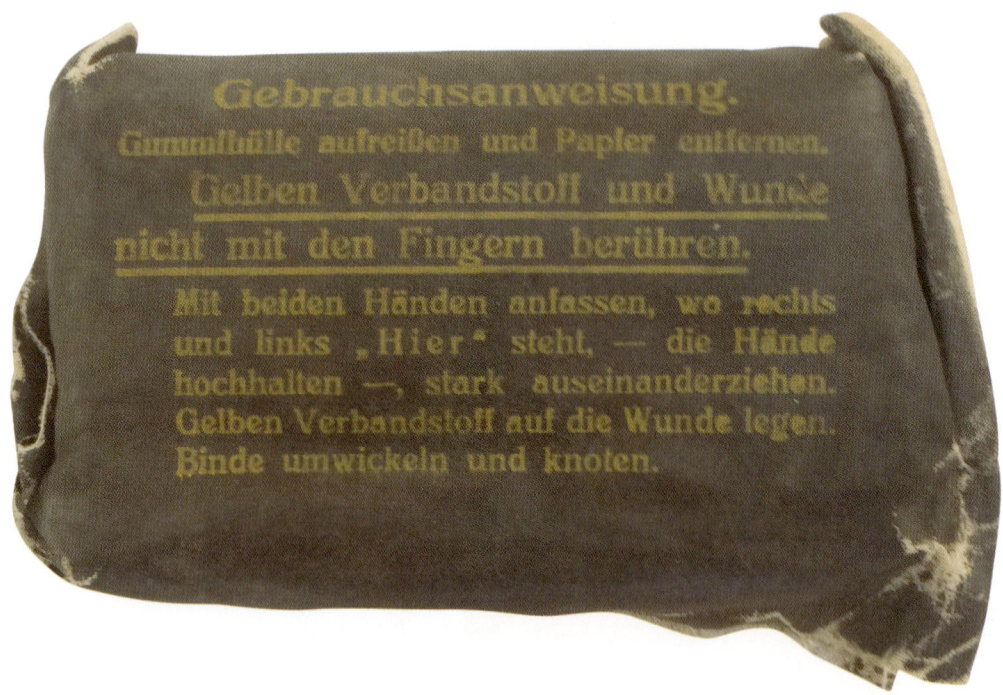

ABOVE and BELOW: Luftwaffe pilots and crew in the battle did not carry as much survival equipment in 1940 as they did later in the war, but this is one essential piece of equipment that could be carried in the inner pocket of the *Fliegerbluse* or trouser pockets along with the gravity knife and possibly some chocolate. These wound dressings are specially impregnated with an ointment for applying to burns and sealed in an oilcloth pouch. This particular one is dated 1939. (Mark Hillier Collection)

LIFESAVING EQUIPMENT

ABOVE and RIGHT: This is a Scho-Ka-Kola tin. It was basically caffeine-infused chocolate, often carried in a tunic or trouser pocket by aircrew as survival rations. Some of the tins that can be found are dated on the front. (Mark Hillier Collection)

Section 6
SERVICE DRESS

Early on, many officers, like the RAF pilots, flew in their service dress with top boots or riding boots rather than flying boots. Some wore flying equipment but many just their uniforms. The *Fliegerbluse* was popular to fly in and it's apparent that most of the NCO aircrew opted for this item during working hours, with service dress or *Tuchrock* being kept for best or when not flying. The badges of rank and other badges worn on uniforms by the Luftwaffe make identification harder than for the RAF who wore simply wings/brevet and rank identification along with maybe VR or A badges on the collars.

Available uniform consisted of three main variants, the *Tuchrock*, *Fliegerbluse* or the *Waffenrock*. These three types were worn by both officers and NCOs, the only difference being the rank insignia and fabric types which are discussed later in this section. The officers would often opt for private purchase items so the garments were of much better quality than the issue equipment. What is clear is that during the Battle of Britain period photos show a variety of dress that was not seen in the RAF.

The Luftwaffe system of rank identification was a combination of collar patches with trade background being identified by the *Waffenfarbe* (branch of service colour) and shoulder rank boards. The braid around the collar patches was also important. The rank shoulder boards for NCOs had a yellow trim, identifying flight crew, and the collar patch and shoulder had silver trim. The officer ranks had silver-embroidered rank identification on the collar and silver piping to the surround. The shoulder tabs were embroidered with silver with pips to identify rank: no pips being Leutnant, one pip being Oberleutnant and two being Hauptman. The bird-type motif, resembling a gull, was used to differentiate the ranks on the collar tab.

Other badges on the Luftwaffe uniform include wound badges which could have been one of three levels, black being the first award. Often pilots and aircrew would also wear the DRL Sports badge which was more of a decoration than a qualification but it recognised a level of fitness. It had been introduced in 1933 and was available in three grades, bronze, silver and gold. Also there was a more general sports award badge that was also worn. Many photos of the period show the various decorations that could be awarded such as the Knight's Cross, Iron Cross First and Second Class etc. These have not been included but are referenced in the photos where shown. Typically the Iron Cross Second Class was indicated by wearing of the ribbon on the edge of the jacket, the First Class award being worn on the left breast pocket.

SERVICE DRESS

ABOVE: A close-up image of the finer material used on a privately tailored officer's *Tuchrock* showing the position of the silver bullion Luftwaffe breast eagle on the right breast with the tail of the eagle over the pocket flap. This photo also shows the silver piping around the collar of an officer and a close up of the Jagdgeschwader 52 badge. The collar rank is that of a Leutnant. (Paul Woodbyrne Collection)

RIGHT: This mannequin shows a typical Luftwaffe Leutnant (equivalent to an RAF pilot officer) service uniform with belt, straight trousers, black shoes, and the officer's brown leather belt which had a two-pronged, pebbled-finished buckle. Light blue shirt with detachable collar and black tie. The rank is denoted by the shoulder epaulettes and collar tabs. Often this was the favoured dress of fighter pilots or the same uniform with riding breeches and top boots or riding boots. This tunic shows the pilot badge under the Iron Cross First Class on the left breast, he also wears the ribbon of the Iron Cross Second Class from the button. On the right breast is the Luftwaffe breast eagle, and he also has a small Jagdgeschwader 52 badge on his right collar. Note the yellow *Waffenfarbe* around the epaulettes and the background colour of the rank badges on the collar denoting flight crew, the silver piping to the edge of the collar denoting commissioned rank. (Paul Woodbyrne Collection)

THE LUFTWAFFE BATTLE OF BRITAIN FIGHTER PILOT'S KITBAG

TUCHROCK OR SERVICE DRESS TUNIC

First entering service in 1937, the *Tuchrock* was a four-pocket, open collar, button-up jacket with four pebble buttons, which was worn with a blue shirt and black tie. The issue garment was made of a blue-grey wool synthetic blend but officers who chose to go to their own tailors had them made from a finer quality wool and gabardine material. The rank was displayed on the collar and the shoulder epaulettes or on the upper left sleeve. Examples of the types of insignia will be covered later in the book. The uniform could also be worn for dress occasions and for this officers would wear a white shirt with it and a brocade belt. For flying duties the jacket was worn with a two-pronged leather belt which had a pebbled buckle although the majority seemed to favour the *Fliegerbluse*.

LEFT: This is a *Tuchrock* of an Unteroffizier (equivalent to RAF sergeant) showing the silver flat braid known as *Tresse* around the collar rank tab denoting NCO rank, with the yellow *Waffenfarbe* of flight crew as piping to the collar and around the epaulets. The national eemblem is the very early first pattern droop-tail eagle worn over the right breast pocket. The NCO would wear the belt shown with the Luftwaffe version of the national insignia on the belt buckle. Later versions were similar but had a black overall appearance to the buckle. The buttons have a very typical silver pebbled appearance. Note the trade badge on the left sleeve which depicts flight personnel who were not entitled to wear the pilot's or air gunner/radio operator's badge. Also shown here is an example of a cuff title, this one Geschwader Horst Wessell was introduced on 24 March 1936 and was worn by members of the *Fliegergeschwader Dortmund* later to become Zerstörergeschwader 26. (Paul Woodbyrne Collection)

SERVICE DRESS

LEFT: This *Tuchrock* shows the rank of an Oberfeldwebel (equivalent to RAF flight sergeant) again an early uniform with the droop-tail eagle on the right breast pocket, NCO *Tresse* around the collar rank tab. (Phil Phillips Collection)

RIGHT: A Gefreiter (equivalent to RAF corporal) pilot's uniform showing the rank chevron on the left sleeve. Note that junior NCO ranks did not have the silver Tresse around the rank on the collar, only the yellow *Waffenfarbe*. This uniform has the Iron Cross First Class on the left breast pocket and the pilot's badge worn under it. The silver wound badge is next to the pilot's badge. The *Tuchrock* had four buttons compared to the *Waffenrock* with five. This was worn with the NCO/enlisted man's belt. (Mark Hillier Collection)

ABOVE: Hauptmann Walter Kienzle shown here wearing his *Tuchrock* or service dress, with breeches and flying boots along with his visor cap. He took command of 5 (Jagd) Trägergruppe 186 at Jever at the end of February 1940. It was intended that II/186 (T) would operate from the aircraft carrier *Graf Zeppelin* but, in the meantime, it carried out normal fighter duties. An experienced pilot, Kienzle, who had previously been *Staffel Kapitän* of 2/Jagdgeschwader 101, was posted to JFS Magdeburg at the end of May 1940, after which his Staffel became 3/Erprobungsgruppe 210, commanded by *Oberleutnant* Otto Hintze. In September 1940, Kienzle was posted to Stab/Jagdgeschwader 26 but was shot down and taken prisoner on the 30th of that month. (Chris Goss)

SERVICE DRESS

FLIEGERBLUSE

This garment was a much simpler affair and was designed as an all-purpose uniform similar in idea to RAF battledress. It was made of a coarse blue-grey wool-synthetic blend and again officers often opted for privately-tailored items made of quality wool and gabardine. It had a single row of concealed plastic buttons down the front and initially it had no pockets but later variants had a slit pocket on each side. Both versions would have appeared during the Battle of Britain and some of the later variants had flapped pockets. Again rank was carried on the collar and shoulder boards. NCO aircrew would wear the jacket with no shirt under it and with a brown leather belt whilst on flying duties (although many discarded the belt) but the officers had to wear this with a blue shirt and black tie.

ABOVE: This is an officer's *Fliegerbluse* for a Hauptmann (equivalent to RAF flight lieutenant). Common and popular with aircrew, they were quite a short fit. Note the concealed buttons, Luftwaffe breast eagle on the right breast, collar rank badge with the yellow *Waffenfarbe* for flight personnel and the officer's silver piping around the collar. This has button-flap pockets which were introduced in 1940. (Paul Woodbyrne Collection)

ABOVE: A Luftwaffe *Fliegerbluse* with shirt and tie being worn with the *Schirmmutze*, pilot's badge and Iron Cross 1st Class. (Mark Hillier Collection)

SERVICE DRESS

ABOVE: A Luftwaffe *Fliegerbluse* being worn with the *Sommermutz*, as was often the case during the summer months of the Battle of Britain. (Mark Hillier Collection)

ABOVE: This is a pre-1940 officer's issue *Fliegerbluse* (after 1940, both officers' and enlisted men's versions were issued with flaps) for a Hauptmann. It is unusual in that it is an officer's version in the coarse material normally associated with the enlisted men's jacket. Most officers chose to have privately-tailored versions in a finer material, but some chose to make do with the issued version in this style of material. The pilot's badge is a version made by C.E. Juncker. Often this was worn with the officer's belt and holster. (Mark Hillier Collection)

RIGHT: The stamp inside shows the jacket to have been manufactured in 1939. The other numbers from top left show back waist of 45cm, top right a neck of 48cm, centre chest size of 108cm, total back on the bottom left of 68cm, and bottom right sleeve length of 67cm. The LBA stamp is for *Luftwaffe Bekleidungs Amt* or Luftwaffe Clothing Administration. (Mark Hillier Collection)

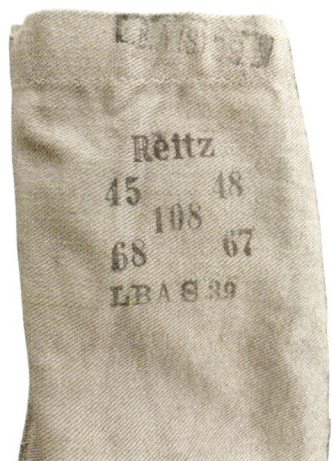

ABOVE: Feldwebel Walter Meudtner of 3/Jagdgeschwader 51 seen here wearing the *Fliegerbluse*, NCO cap and long trousers. On his feet he wears leather marching boots. Note the silver braid around the collar indicating NCO rank. Also, he wears a cloth version of the pilot' badge on the left breast pocket. Meudtner flew throughout the Battle of Britain but claimed no victories. On 26 September 1940, Meudtner was flying with his *Staffel Kapitän*, Oberleutnant Richard Leppla, when they bounced two Hurricanes over the Channel. The RAF fighters are believed to have been flown by Flight Lieutenant G.R. Edge and Pilot Officer W.M.C. Samolinski of 253 Squadron. Both Hurricanes were shot down; Edge was wounded and Samolinski killed. Meudtner, flying Bf 109E-4 Wk Nr 5369, also failed to return. As there were no witnesses to the destruction of the Hurricanes, they were not claimed. (Chris Goss)

THE LUFTWAFFE BATTLE OF BRITAIN FIGHTER PILOT'S KITBAG

LEFT and BELOW: A Luftwaffe officer's uniform/equipment carrier which is dated 1940 on the leather straps. Inside are a number of leather loops stitched to the rigid top board to hold coat hangers. This was carried using leather shoulder straps on the back. (Mark Hillier Collection)

SERVICE DRESS

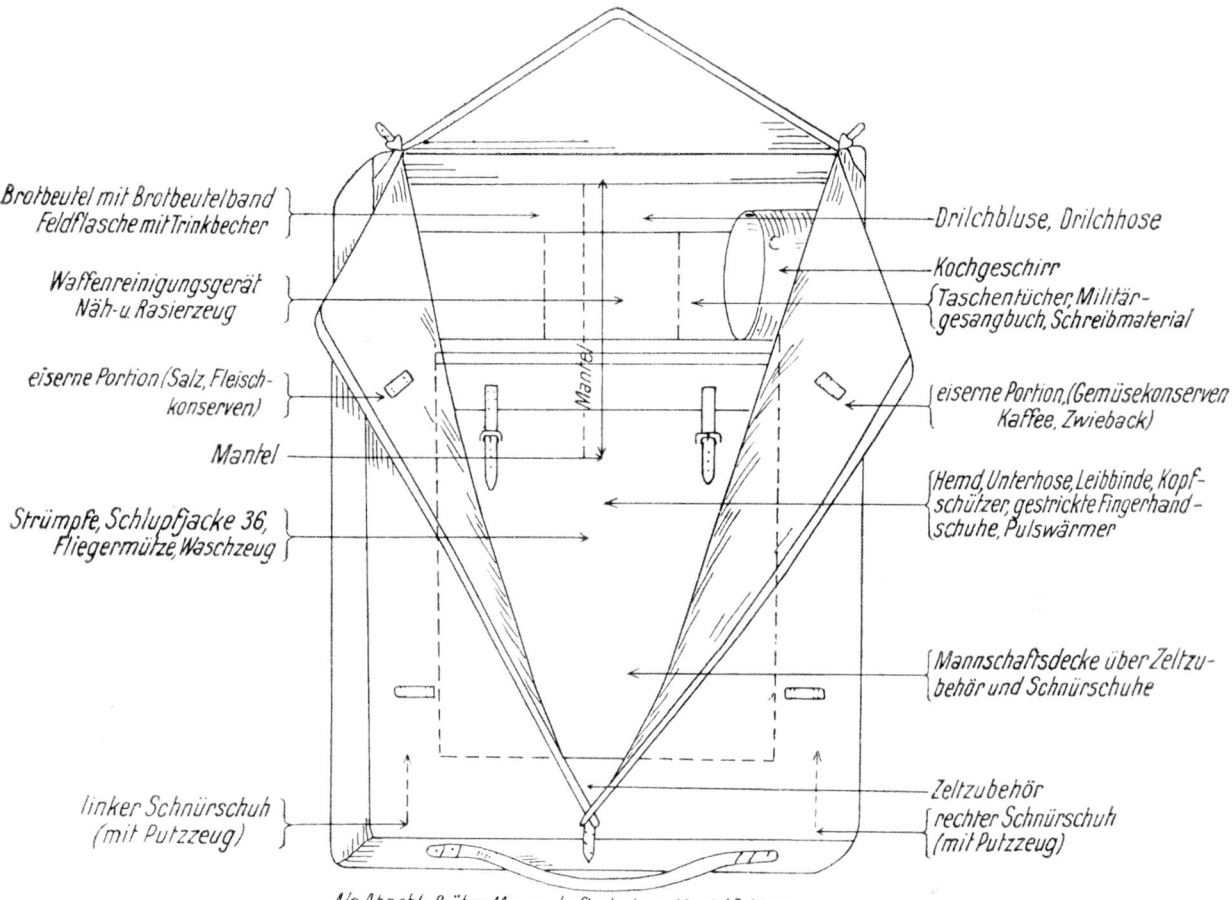

ABOVE: A page from the Handbook of the Luftwaffe (which is covered later) showing the correct manner for packing a uniform/equipment carrier. (Mark Hillier Collection)

WAFFENROCK

The idea behind this garment was that it would replace the previous two items of clothing. Introduced in 1938 it looked very similar in design to the *Tuchrock*, the differences being that it had five buttons on the front and the collar was different in the fact that it could be left open to wear with a shirt or tie, or could be buttoned up and therefore no shirt would be required. It had a five-button front, the buttons having a white aluminium pebble-surfaced appearance. This differed to the four-button front of the *Tuchrock*. However it was not as popular and the previous two items continued to be worn throughout the Battle of Britain period and are seen in the majority of period photographs.

THE LUFTWAFFE BATTLE OF BRITAIN FIGHTER PILOT'S KITBAG

ABOVE: A page from the Handbook of the Luftwaffe (which is covered later) depicting items of Luftwaffe uniform. (Mark Hillier Collection)

SERVICE DRESS

SUMMER TUNIC

Authorised for summer wear only in the European Theatre, this was exactly the same as the *Tuchrock* but made of white linen, gabardine or cotton. Key differences included the omission of the 3mm silver braid around the collar. The breast eagle was a pin-backed metal item and the collar and even the shoulder boards were all easily removable. The idea was that with easily removable insignia etc, it would be easier and quicker to clean. It was often worn with an officer's brocade belt to complete the dashing look of a fighter pilot.

ABOVE: Luftwaffe Oberleutnant's summer tunic. The removable eagle in metal with a pin back can be seen on the right breast. Note the additional loops sewn into the jacket for pilot's badge, Iron Cross etc. (Paul Woodbyrne Collection)

LEFT: Luftwaffe Oberleutnant's summer tunic worn with the brocade belt. (Paul Woodbyrne Collection)

87

THE LUFTWAFFE BATTLE OF BRITAIN FIGHTER PILOT'S KITBAG

SERVICE SHIRTS

The requirements for wearing shirts under the service uniform were that normally a blue shirt was to be worn with a black tie, but a white shirt and black tie could be worn, for example with the *Tuchrock* which was appropriate as walking-out dress for all Luftwaffe ranks. A white shirt with stiff collar and black tie could be worn with the service tunic as informal and formal full dress for NCOs and informal and formal daytime full dress for officers.

LEFT: This is a Luftwaffe blue shirt worn under the service uniform and with a black tie. Usually found with a detachable collar but this particular one has it sewn on by the owner. Very rare to find as they rarely survived the war and those that did were worn to bits after it. (Paul Woodbyrne Collection)

RIGHT: The label of the shirt translates as 'Sales Department of the Luftwaffe, Berlin'. (Paul Woodbyrne Collection)

SERVICE DRESS

SERVICE TROUSERS

The service trousers were of a straight cut for all of the above items. Matching trousers were worn with the exception that officers were allowed to wear blue-grey riding breeches. It is clear from some period photos that NCO pilots would often disregard regulations and also opted for the riding breeches.

ABOVE: A pair of officer's-issue riding breeches showing the flaring at the waist and thigh and narrowing to the calf They normally had lace-up bottoms, but these are more unusual with a zip bottom. (Phil Phillips Collection).

THE LUFTWAFFE BATTLE OF BRITAIN FIGHTER PILOT'S KITBAG

LUFTWAFFE CABLE-KNIT SWEATER

Photographs exist of several fighter pilots wearing a button-fronted cable-knit sweater. These are very difficult to find in collections today. Knitted in a light blue-grey coloured yarn with a crew neck, it had a tightly-knitted waistband and wrist sections.

LEFT: These cable-knit sweaters, which were favoured by some fighter pilots, are very hard to find. Lots of the kit, such as shirts and jumpers, that were of use after the war were worn until they fell apart so are much more difficult to find. (Paul Woodbyrne Collection)

SERVICE DRESS

ABOVE: Oberleutnant Karl Lommel, the *Staffel Kapitän* of 1/Jagdgeschwader 52, standing on the wing wearing his cable-knit sweater, breeches and early Hoffman brown leather and suede boots. He looks on as a kitten plays on the cowling of a Bf 109E-1 at Lachen-Speyerdorf in early 1940. The Running Boar emblem of 1/Jagdgeschwader 52 was red and blue, with a black boar. Lommel took command of 1 Staffel in March 1940 and was not posted away until he was given temporary command of 1/Jagdgeschwader 52 in November 1941 following the wounding of Oberleutnant Karl-Heinz Leesmann. By this time Lommel had shot down three aircraft. In mid-1942 he was posted away to be a fighter pilot instructor. It is believed he survived the war. (Chris Goss)

NON-FLYING HEADGEAR

Much like the opposition, the Luftwaffe had two types of uniform hat, a peaked cap and a forage cap, the difference being that both were available to all ranks with minor differences. In period photos you can often see a strange mix-and-match going on: for example some fighter pilots would wear the summer cap with the *Fliegerbluse* as a preference. The majority of NCO aircrew, it seems, opted to wear the forage cap with their uniform.

Schirmmutze
This peaked cap worn by all ranks with a blue-grey top, with a black ribbed mohair cap band with a black shiny peak. For officers this had silver cap cords with matt silver buttons to hold them in place.

THE LUFTWAFFE BATTLE OF BRITAIN FIGHTER PILOT'S KITBAG

The cap was piped in silver aluminium, the peak being shiny black with a green underside. The insignia were normally of hand-embroidered silver wire and sewn onto the hat. The higher ranks of General and above had gold coloured chords and the emblems again embroidered in gold. These hats were manufactured to a much higher quality than those worn by the NCOs. The NCO hat was much simpler with the metal emblem being affixed with metal prongs, still with the Luftwaffe national emblem at the top, oak-leaf wreath and stylized wings, all silver-coloured pressed aluminium. The NCO cap also had a black patent leather chinstrap.

ABOVE: A saddle-form officer's peaked cap, with higher centre section, which came into service after 1935. Note the droop-tail eagle indicating an early example. This is the style of cap most often seen in photos from the period. (Phil Phillips Collection)

ABOVE: A nice example of an early peaked cap for officers, this one with a small hand-embroidered Luftwaffe eagle in silvered aluminium wire thread and manufactured in Berlin, dating to 1935. Note the silver wire thread edging around the cap which on the NCO cap is a yellow *Waffenfarbe*. (Mark Hillier Collection)

RIGHT: A 1939-dated NCO peaked cap dated 1939. Note the difference from the officer's cap in that this version has yellow *Waffenfarbe* piping of the air branch and metal insignia which are fixed with prongs through the front. (Mark Hillier Collection)

SERVICE DRESS

ABOVE: This highly-decorated officer, who has just been awarded the Iron Cross Second Class, is Oberleutnant Wilhelm Balthasar, the *Staffel Kapitän* of 1/Jagdgeschwader 1. He received the honour, which accompanied those he gained in Spain with J/88, on 23 September 1939. He stands in front of White 1 which also carries the *Staffel Kapitän*'s pennant on the radio mast. Balthasar would be awarded the Knight's Cross with Oakleaves and, with his score standing at forty-seven, was shot down and killed on 3 July 1941 when commanding Jagdgeschwader 2. Here he wears his service tunic, breeches and high boots of black leather, probably private purchase. Note also he wears his brown belt and cross strap: the cross strap was abolished in February 1940. He wears a saucer-shaped peaked cap or *Schirmmutzen* rather than the saddle form with the higher front peak more recognisable from the Battle of Britain period. (Chris Goss)

THE LUFTWAFFE BATTLE OF BRITAIN FIGHTER PILOT'S KITBAG

Sommermutze *or Summer Cap*

These white-topped caps were virtually identical to the *Schirmmutze* and were mainly issued before the war. Worn with the white summer uniform, they was not issued after the start of the hostilities, but it was still permitted to be worn between the dates of 1 April to 30 September. Made from a diagonally-patterned cotton drill, the NCO version had a yellow *Waffenfarbe* band around the top and bottom edge of the black Mohair band, again with aluminium alloy badges. A number of period images do show aircrew wearing this with the blue-grey uniform as mentioned previously.

LEFT: An NCO/enlisted man's version of the summer peaked cap showing the white top, yellow *Waffenfarbe* and aluminium alloy badge rather than the officer's silver wire thread. Also the black chin strap. (Paul Woodbyrne Collection)

RIGHT: An officer's version of the summer peaked cap, this time made from a white cotton fabric and displaying the saddle form shape. Note the officers' silver wire thread of the badges and no silver piping around the top edge of the cap as per regulations for the standard officer's cap. (Paul Woodbyrne Collection)

SERVICE DRESS

ABOVE LEFT and RIGHT: Another variation of an NCO's summer peak cap, with a traditional saddle form top. (Mark Hillier Collection)

Fliegermutze

Many aircrew opted for the fore-and-aft style forage cap as day-to-day wear as it was easier to carry in your flying equipment or put in a pocket, although it was a standard issue item. The Luftwaffe did have a choice of both for officers and NCOs, whereas in the RAF the NCO only had the forage cap and no issue service cap. It was of a blue-grey material, the officers often opting for higher-quality yarns. The *Fliegermutze* had the Luftwaffe National Emblem centrally stitched on the middle seam

RIGHT: The flyer's cap was introduced after 1935. This officer's version shown here lying flat gives an idea of how easy it was to carry and maybe fold up and put in the pocket of a flying suit. Here you can also see the silver piping of a 3mm aluminium chord around the edge, which gave easy identification of officer rank. (Simon Lannoy Collection)

at the front of the cap above the turn up. Below this and again central was the *Reichskokarde*. The outer ring of this varied: for NCOs this was in grey cotton yarn but for officers this would be in silver wire, while for the top ranks of general and above it would be gilt wire. The same principal applied to the Luftwaffe National Emblem, the NCOs' one being grey machined cotton yarn, officers up to the rank of Oberst hand-embroidered silvered aluminium and generals upwards in Gilt. The *Fliegermutze* was piped around the edge of the turn-up for officers with a 3mm wide silver cord, again gilt for generals and above.

LEFT: This close-up shot of the front of the cap shows the national emblem and the Luftwaffe eagle in hand-embroidered silver wire. Ranks of general and above were in gold thread. (Simon Lannoy Collection)

BELOW: Leutnant Jochen Schypek of 3/Jagdgeschwader 76 photographed wearing his service uniform with blue-grey shirt, black tie and flyer's cap. Note the silver piping around the edge of the cap denoting officer rank. He stands with his mechanic in front of his Bf 109E-3, Wk Nr 1266, Yellow 13. (Chris Goss)

SERVICE DRESS

ABOVE LEFT: This is the NCO/enlisted man's version of the flyer's cap. Note the coarser material, no piping and machine-embroidered emblems. (Paul Woodbyrne Collection)

ABOVE RIGHT: Manufacturer's markings in the NCO/enlisted man's version of the flyer's cap. (Paul Woodbyrne Collection)

BELOW: An unusual and rare example of an NCO and other ranks' *Fliegermutze* with yellow *Waffenfarbe* (branch of service colour) which was later discontinued. This example is dated 1940. (Simon Lannoy Collection)

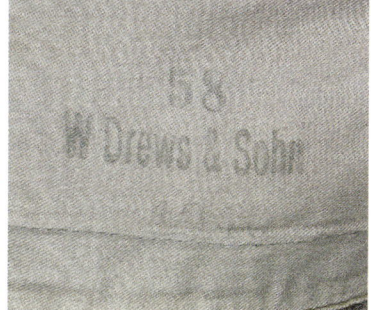

THE LUFTWAFFE BATTLE OF BRITAIN FIGHTER PILOT'S KITBAG

SERVICE SHOES/BOOTS

The aircrew wore black leather lace-up shoes or sometimes brown or black leather top boots, which look like knee-length riding boots. The whole image with the leather jacket, riding breeches and knee length boots for officers gave the appearance of a gallant hunter riding out to battle! However, this practice was eventually forbidden and pilots and aircrew were told to wear the flying boots issued.

LEFT: An example of officer's black leather high boots. These are a private purchase version and fighter pilots early in the war chose to wear these with riding breeches rather than the issue flying boots until an order came out forbidding their wear due to the difficulty encountered and injury caused to aircrew that were burnt when trying to remove them. (Phil Phillips Collection)

BELOW: These marching boots were standard issue to NCO aircrew and enlisted men. They were made of black leather with pull straps on the inside of both sides. Often seen worn by aircrew with the *Fliegerbluse*. (Paul Woodbyrne Collection)

SERVICE DRESS

BELTS

For officers this was a brown leather service belt with a two-pronged open-claw buckle whilst the non-commissioned aircrew wore the leather waist belt with a metal box buckle with the Luftwaffe emblem on the front. During the Battle of Britain period this was silver in colour or natural metal finish. The belt for both can be seen being worn over the one-piece summer flying suit and with the *Fliegerbluse* on operational sorties.

ABOVE: The belts often carry a stamp with the date on them and can sometimes be found with a unit stamp, in this example Kampfgeschwader 155 which later became Kampfgeschwader 55, dating the belt to before 1940. (Mark Hillier Collection)

ABOVE: The NCO/enlisted man's belt, the buckle shown here in detail. The belt itself measured approximately 4.5cm wide and was of black leather. The buckle was constructed in aluminium with a pebbled finish and with the eagle emblem in the centre. This photo shows the belt supporting a P.08 holster, also in black leather. (Mark Hillier Collection)

RIGHT: An officer's belt made of brown leather, wider than the NCO/enlisted man's belt with a rectangular buckle with two open prongs. The buckle itself being pebbled matt-white metal with slightly rounded corners. (Mark Hillier Collection)

SOCKS

The socks that were issued were of a calf-length grey woollen variety and these were issued to all male Luftwaffe personnel. White knitted rings around the top of the sock indicated the size, of which four were available.

SPORTS CLOTHING

The German military was big on sport and so all personnel were issued with sports vests in a white cotton material, which had the Luftwaffe version of the national emblem below the neck opening. Also issued were sports shorts, running shoes and bathing trunks, amongst other items that were allowed by private purchase such as the tracksuit.

ABOVE: Though not a Battle of Britain period photograph (note the *Tropenheim* he is wearing), this is a rare image showing an individual wearing examples of the Luftwaffe's sports vest. (Chris Goss)

SERVICE DRESS

ABOVE and RIGHT: A nice double-decal M35 helmet showing on one side the national tricolour which was discontinued on helmets after March 1940 and on the other side the second pattern Luftwaffe national emblem which began to appear in 1937. (Simon Lannoy Collection)

STEEL HELMET

The M35 or 'Model 35' steel helmet, introduced from January 1936, was a step up in design from the previous M18 helmet. It offered better protection, was easier to sight weapons and use optics while wearing, and the upturned skirts also gave better hearing over the earlier helmets. These were painted in a blue-grey finish and had the Luftwaffe National Emblem on the left, and the national colours on the right side of the helmet.

GAS MASK

All arms of the German forces were issued with a gas mask, but for the Luftwaffe this was not for use in the air but in case of gas attack on the ground. Due to the widespread use of gas in the First World War, the Germans developed the M1915 and M1917 gas mask which evolved into the Reichswehr-era M24 and eventually the M30 and M38 which was the main type issued in the Second World War. It came with a canister and accessories.

ABOVE: An early M30 model gas mask dated 1937 dated with a first-model short canister. These were not specific to the Luftwaffe. (CS Militaria)

GREATCOATS, CLOTH AND LEATHER VARIETY

The cloth greatcoat worn by both officers and NCOs in the Luftwaffe was exactly the same, a style established back in 1935 for use in cold weather. A blue-grey colour with a button-up front designed to be worn with either the neck open, the top three buttons left undone or to be buttoned fully. Officers would wear it with a belt. The buttons are the same style as for the *Tuchrock* and rank was again shown on the collar and the greatcoat had shoulder patches, *Waffenfarbe* differentiating the branch of the individual. The Luftwaffe also allowed private purchase leather greatcoats which pretty much complied with the same style as the cloth version, in a fine-grained blue-grey leather with similar buttons to the cloth version although pre-1937 versions can be found with blue grey plastic versions. Officers were also allowed to have a rubberized top coat in a similar colour and cut.

SERVICE DRESS

RIGHT: An example of an officer's private purchase leather greatcoat which was very similar in design to the cloth variety. The shoulder boards are detachable and secured with a pebbled button. Often worn with the officers' belt. (Paul Woodbyrne Collection)

ABOVE: Two pilots of 5/ Jagdgeschwader 27 pictured on their airfield at Montreuil during the early part of the Battle of Britain. The individual on the right is Oberleutnant Erwin Daig. On 9 September 1940, Daig, at the controls of a Bf 109E-1, was shot down in combat over West Sussex. That afternoon he was part of the escort for a large formation of bombers whose target was the London docks. On the approach his Bf 109 was hit and began to lose speed. After the bombers had delivered their deadly cargos upon London, Daig found himself intercepted by two British fighters and his already-damaged aircraft was struck again. He dived away from his pursers and tried to reach a bank of broken cloud which was at a height of about 9,000 feet. 'Before I reached the safety of this cloud,' he later recalled, 'one of my attackers caught up with me and again opened fire. Once again, I felt the shock of more hits, at which point I put my 'plane into yet another dive. This time I kept going until I was almost at ground level, when I headed straight for France, trying to escape by flying at low level.' Daig never made it home. The British fighters pursued him relentlessly and his Messerschmitt took more hits. 'By now my 'plane had started to smoke, and I was having trouble seeing. I threw back my cockpit hood to see if this would help, but all that happened was that the engine just died. I then saw a gently rising slope, similar to a meadow, that was profusely covered with old lorries. I quickly lost speed and then the 'plane hit the ground. The chase was finally over!' The Bf 109 came to ground on a small private landing strip used by the residents of nearby Parham House before the war (it is today the home of Southdown Gliding Club). The lorries Daig referred to, along with abandoned cars and farming implements, had been scattered across the field as anti-glider and anti-invasion measures. Daig also recounted his first hours as a prisoner of war: 'I was well treated . . . an English officer asked me if I had any firearms, to which I replied "no". I was then taken from the crash site to a nearby army base where I was shown to the commanding officer who offered me a glass of whiskey.' Both of these officers are wearing private purchase leather greatcoats, the officer on the left with his service peaked cap showing the high peak of the saddle form variety, Oberleutnant Erwin Daig wears his *Fliegermutzen* or flyer's cap. (Historic Military Press)

SERVICE DRESS

RIGHT: This identity tag belonged to Oberfeldwebel Kurt Rochel who was a Condor Legion pilot. He later went on to fly the Bf 110 with Zestörergeschwader 26 during the Battle of Britain. He was shot down on 2 September 1940 and became a PoW. Note the tag only contains the squadron details and an identity number that only the Luftwaffe would know. (Phil Phillips Collection)

IDENTITY TAGS

These were stamped aluminium tags with a perforation down the centre of the oval disk with the information about the individual stamped on both halves. This did not contain a name, purely a service number and unit information. This meant the Germans had to keep exceptionally good records in order to identify casualties. This was worn around the neck on a 40cm-long piece of grey woollen thread.

SERVICE PISTOL

Some of the Luftwaffe crews flew with a sidearm, and both officers and NCO aircrew alike carried pistols such as the Luger P.08 or Walther P38 pistol, amongst others. One pilot who tried to evade capture after being shot down and bailing out was Unteroffizier Siegfried Becker of 1/Zerstörergeschwader 2: 'We both came down by parachute unwounded but my Bordfunker broke his ankle on landing. He was on one side of a railway cutting and I the other. In the distance I saw Home Guardsmen so I tried getting away by running along the railway line. However I soon saw British soldiers on a bridge over the line about 200–300m away. I was captured, disarmed and taken to a private house.'[16]

THE LUFTWAFFE BATTLE OF BRITAIN FIGHTER PILOT'S KITBAG

Other handguns were available, such as the Walther PP which was the forerunner of the PPK. Another type available was the Mauser Model 1934. Not all felt that carrying a pistol was worthwhile, as Unteroffizier Willi Ghesla of 1 Staffel of 2/Jagdgeschwader 53 who had been issued with a Walther PP explained: 'Four of us, Herbert Tzschoppe, Werner Karl, Heinrich Hohnisch and myself left our pistols in our accommodation as we felt they were useless if we were ever shot down. We had this mutual agreement and would say "if I am shot down keep my pistol". I was not to know that within a month, I would have a total of four.'[17]

Oberleutnant Jochen Schypek also chose not to fly with his service pistol, as after capture the Captain in charge of the arresting soldiers was surprised to find out; 'What followed was rather funny. The captain pulled out a check list and registered my name and rank first and drew the automatic blanks when asking for unit, home base etc. Next he wanted to have my pistol and was shocked that I only had my signal pistol to surrender. How could I enter enemy territory practically unarmed? I told him my "arms" were in the aircraft wings and fuselage and in the narrow Messerschmitt cockpit a pistol holster was too much bother. I had to agree that by flying without a sidearm, I had violated Luftwaffe regulations.'[18]

ABOVE: Known by many as the Luger, this was officially the Model P.08 pistol which had a magazine holding eight rounds of 9mm ammunition. Most of the Luftwaffe versions of this pistol were manufactured by Krieghoff, with somewhere in the region of 14,000 being made by this firm up until 1945. (Simon Lannoy Collection)

BELOW: Oberleutnant Anton Stangl of 5/Jagdgeschwader 54 seen here wearing his flyer's blouse and officer's belt with sidearm. (Chris Goss)

SERVICE DRESS

RIGHT: A hard-shell leather holster in black leather worn by NCOs/enlisted men. It was provided with an extra magazine pocket stitched along the forward edge. These are always dated on the rear and have the manufacturer's details along with an acceptance stamp. (Simon Lannoy Collection)

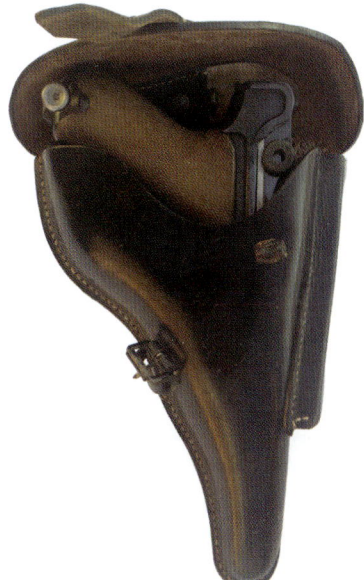

BELOW: A period photograph of a Bf 110 crewman standing next to his crashed aircraft somewhere in France, wearing a one-piece summer flight suit, belt and pistol holster. (Chris Goss)

SERVICE PISTOL HOLSTER

The aircrew would wear a brown or black leather pistol holster on the belt, worn on the left-hand side, designed for the type of pistol they were carrying such as the Walther PP or P.08. These were marked with a manufacturer's stamp and date on the rear.

THE LUFTWAFFE BATTLE OF BRITAIN FIGHTER PILOT'S KITBAG

BADGES AND *WAFFENFARBE*

The Luftwaffe had a wide variety of trade badges to identify their personnel and with the mix of awards, national insignia and rank identification, it makes its uniforms much more interesting to collect and research. For flying badges there were many different makers, even wound badges were manufactured by a variety of companies which were all marked on the rear of the badge.

Flying personnel were easily identifiable by the *Waffenfarbe* on their collar patches and epaulettes. In true German style nothing was left to chance and everything given a code, place and identification. In comparison the RAF uniform really only had rank, flying badges and occasionally an award such as a small Distinguished Flying Cross or other medal ribbon over the left pocket: very conservative.

ABOVE LEFT: This photo illustrates the rank insignia of a Gefreiter showing the yellow *Waffenfarbe* of flight personnel as a background. As seen on many of the other photographs this colour was evident on collar ranks, piping on NCO peaked caps, shoulder boards etc. (Mark Hillier Collection)

ABOVE RIGHT: This is an Oberleutnant's shoulder board showing the *Waffenfarbe* behind the woven silver chord. Again, the NCO shoulder board also had yellow *Waffenfarbe*. (Mark Hillier Collection)

SERVICE DRESS

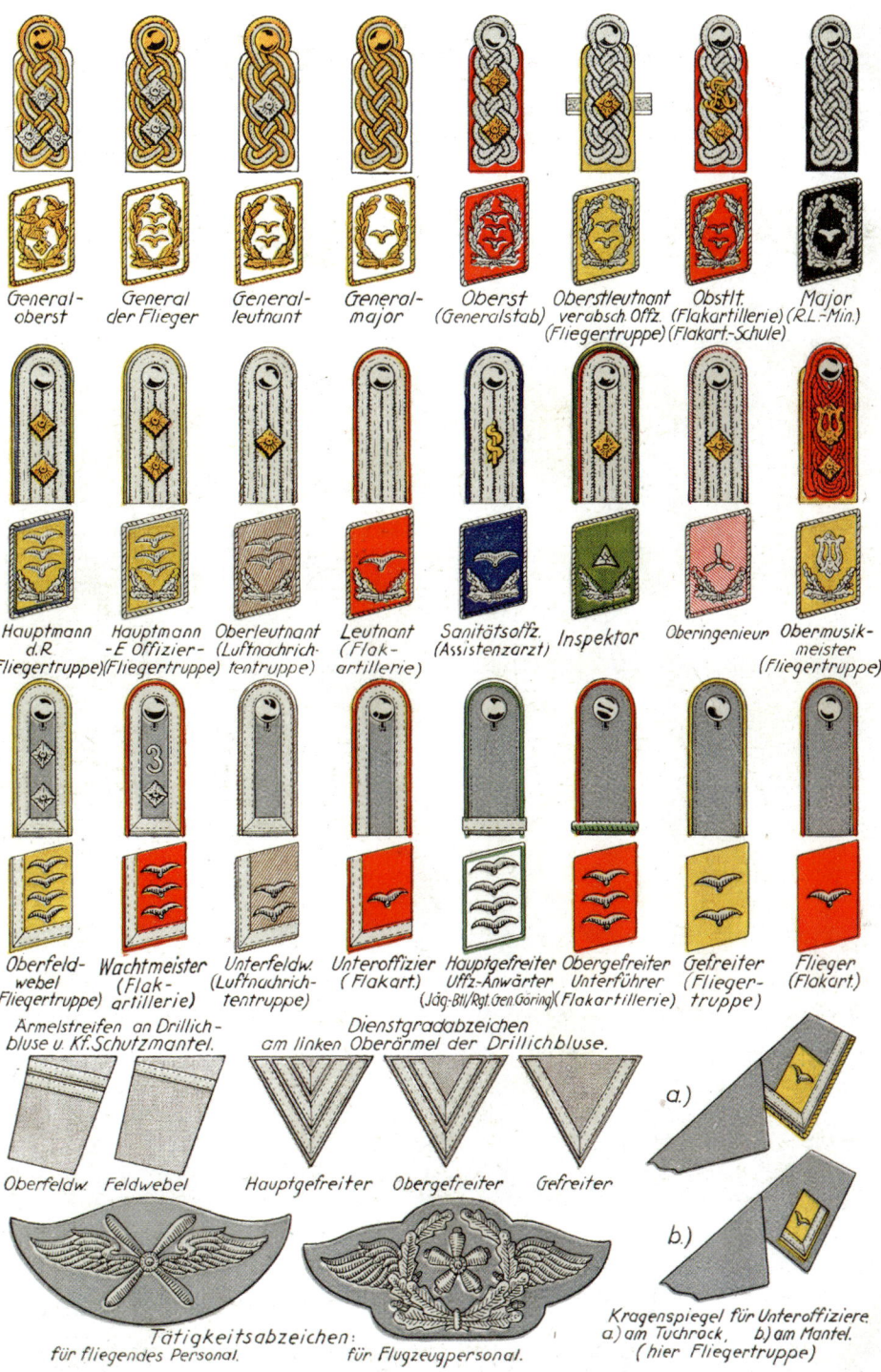

ABOVE: A page from the Handbook of the Luftwaffe (which is covered later) that detailed various rank badges and insignia. (Mark Hillier Collection)

THE LUFTWAFFE BATTLE OF BRITAIN FIGHTER PILOT'S KITBAG

Waffenfarbe

A colour reference system was introduced to the Luftwaffe similar to that of the army to provide backing colours or piping to insignia and uniforms so that its wearer's branch of service could be identified. Flying personnel wore yellow *Waffenfarbe* whereas administrative staff wore dark green.

The National Emblem on Uniforms

On all Luftwaffe uniforms the national emblem is found on the top of the right-hand breast pocket. For the cloth uniforms this was either hand embroidered or for the summer uniform this

LEFT: The national emblem, white metal and pin back type worn on both private purchase leather jackets or on the summer uniform. (Mark Hillier Collection)

An early droop-tail eagle on the Luftwaffe national insignia, on the above, and a rare gold General's version on the right. (Ken Aitken Collection)

SERVICE DRESS

LEFT: An example of the woven national emblem, this one showing the characteristics of an early droop-tail eagle, again worn on the right breast pocket, overlapping the pocket flap. (Mark Hillier Collection)

BELOW LEFT: This Gefreiter pilot wears a typical *Fliegerbluse* with the national emblem and cloth pilot's badge on the left breast, and as well as his collar rank, he wears a single chevron on the left sleeve. (Mark Hillier)

ABOVE RIGHT: Unteroffizier Kurt Sauer of 9/Jagdgeschwader 53 poses for the camera in early 1940 on what is believed to be a Bf 109E-3. He wears a *Fliegerbluse* and his NCO braid can be seen on the collar; note that he is not wearing a national emblem on the right breast: this did not become standard until October 1940. Note the distinctive camouflage and the size of the *Pik As* emblem. Sauer would survive the Battle of Britain, though he was reported missing near the Molodechno region of Belarus just after shooting down his fifth enemy aircraft on the evening of 27 June 1941. At the time he was flying a Bf 109F-2, which, with the Wk Nr 6689, was coded Yellow 4+I. (Chris Goss)

could be a cast aluminium badge with a pin back which was also used by some on the private purchase leather jacket. The emblem for the Luftwaffe is an eagle with outstretched wings as if flying, clutching a swastika in its left talon. The early versions have a very noticeable droop tail on the eagle.

Flying Badges

The Luftwaffe pilot badge was introduced at the behest of the commander-in-chief of the Luftwaffe Hermann Göring on 26 March 1936 and consists of a swooping eagle clutching a swastika in its talons. The eagle is mounted on a wreath of half laurel and half oak leaves and was worn below the left breast pocket on the uniform. The pilot badge can be found in materials of different quality. Aluminium, nickel-silver, plated tombak, plated alloy and lacquered zinc were all used. Pre- and early war versions tend to be made in high-quality nickel and tombak, and are of multi-part construction with a pin for fastening at the rear.

The pilot badge is always finished with a dark oxidized eagle and silver wreath. The makers mark is normally on the rear and include such makers as C.E Junker, IMME and F.W. Assmann und Sohn, amongst many others.

There was also a cloth version of the flying badge. Luftwaffe aircrew were often told to take off the metal badges before operational sorties for a couple of reasons, one being that they might damage the life jacket and secondly to sanitize the uniform if captured. The badge was issued on completion of flying training and at the same time the recipient would receive his citation and flying licence. Often if aircrew were flying with any badges these were often confiscated or liberated for souvenirs by their capturers as confirmed by an account by Oberleutnant Günter Buesgen of 1/Jagdgeschwader 52 who was shot down on 12 October 1940: 'I came down safely by parachute and was welcomed by the Home Guard. They removed my gun (and my pilot's badge and Iron Cross) and I was taken to a local hospital.'[19]

ABOVE LEFT: This is a Luftwaffe pilot's badge with pin back, manufactured by F.W. Assman. Its shows considerable signs of wear and tear to the extent that the owner has had it re-riveted after the eagle broke. (Mark Hillier Collection)

ABOVE MIDDLE: The reverse of the badge showing the field repair and also the 'A' indicating the maker being Assman. Note also that the owner has engraved his initials on the back of the eagle and coloured them in red. (Mark Hillier Collection)

ABOVE RIGHT: Many pilots opted to wear the cloth version of the pilot's badge. This particular version has a padded back. (Mark Hillier Collection)

SERVICE DRESS

ABOVE: Three variants of a pilot's badge showing the slight variations in manufacture. The first example was made by Juncker, the second by P. Meybauer and the last by Freiderich Linden. (Ken Aitken Collection)

THE LUFTWAFFE BATTLE OF BRITAIN FIGHTER PILOT'S KITBAG

Other Flying Brevets

The only other badge would have been worn by the air gunner in the Bf 110 twin-engined fighter. This was the Radio Operator/Air Gunner's Badge which came into existence on 26 March 1936. This is very similar in construction to the pilot badge but the eagle carries lightning bolts with a Swastika on the base of the wreath. The Radio Operator/Air Gunner's Badge was awarded after they completed two months training or had taken part in at least five operational flights, but if a gunner was wounded during an operational flight, the badge could be awarded and worn earlier.

Aircrew NCOs who were not qualified for the pilot badge or Radio Operator/Air Gunner's Bage were identifiable by a cloth patch which had a four-bladed propeller with a set of wings on it, worn on the left sleeve. These were matt grey embroidery on a blue-grey backing cloth.

ABOVE LEFT: This is the Radio Operator/Air Gunners' Badge worn by the crew member in the rear seat of the Bf110. Note the difference in that the eagle is clutching lightning bolts with its talons and not holding the swastika. It is quite a drastically different design and easy to identify. (Mark Hillier Collection)

ABOVE RIGHT: The reverse of the badge showing the pin back and the maker's details on the reverse of the eagle, this badge being manufactured by C.E. Junker of Berlin. (Mark Hillier Collection)

OPPOSITE ABOVE LEFT: The cloth version of the Radio Operator/Air Gunners' Badge. In due course a separate badge was brought in for air gunners. (Paul Woodbyrne Collection)

OPPOSITE ABOVE RIGHT: This badge is a trade badge worn on the left sleeve for aircrew who had not yet met the qualification requirements for the award of the pilot's or Radio Operator/Air Gunners' Badge. (Paul Woodbyrne Collection)

SERVICE DRESS

Rank Insignia

Luftwaffe rank insignia is identifiable on the collar patches of the uniform which had an underlay depicting the colour of the branch of service. The wings on the officer's patches would be embroidered sliver wire gulls whereas for an NCO these would normally be white metal. Rank on flying suits, in particular the *Sommerfliegerkombi*, are found on the arm around the elbow area. Luftwaffe NCOs would also wear a rank chevron on the service dress tunic, *Fliegerbluse* and greatcoat. These were silver chevrons sewn on to a blue-grey cloth backing. Of course it is not that simple and the Luftwaffe had identification for officer candidates and NCO candidates which have not been included here. Examples of the style of rank have been shown but not the complete set which is much better covered in established texts such as Roger Bender's book.

RIGHT: The shoulder rank boards of an Oberfeldwebel showing the silver *Tresse* and the yellow *Waffenfarbe*. (Mark Hillier Collection)

THE LUFTWAFFE BATTLE OF BRITAIN FIGHTER PILOT'S KITBAG

ABOVE: A rank patch as worn on the summer flying suit, this one being a Feldwebel's. (Paul Woodbyrne Collection)

LEFT: The shoulder rank and collar rank of an Oberleutnant, which was the equivalent of an RAF flying officer. (Mark Hillier Collection)

RIGHT: An extremely rare set of uniform insignia to a Luftwaffe General and appropriate to the ranks of General Der Flieger. The set comprises a General's breast eagle and a matching pair of collar tabs. (Simon Lannoy Collection)

SERVICE DRESS

Verwundetenabzeichen, *Wound Badge*

This badge was first awarded in the First World War and had three classes. The black third class was awarded to those wounded once or twice, the silver second class for being wounded three or four times and the gold first class for being wounded five or more times but could also be awarded posthumously. Made by many manufacturers with various pins and materials, the rear of the badge normally shows the maker's mark or code such as 'L11' and these can be identified. The badge was worn under the left breast pocket on the service uniform and attached through sewn loops into the material.

ABOVE LEFT and RIGHT: A cased Silver Wound Badge with a pin back showing the maker's mark number 30 Hauptmunzamt of Vienna. These were normally worn on the left side, under the pocket. (Mark Hillier Collection)

RIGHT: A Wound Badge in black for a first wound. This is of pressed construction with pin back, from the maker L11 Wilhelm Deumer. (Mark Hillier Collection)

THE LUFTWAFFE BATTLE OF BRITAIN FIGHTER PILOT'S KITBAG

Cuff Titles

A number of cuff titles were given approval to be worn by fighter crews from 1937 on the left sleeve. Some were worn to honour personnel or Luftwaffe units and some to identify certain elite units but also campaign cuff titles were awarded. One that would have been worn during the Battle of

LEFT: A commemorative cuff title worn by Jagdgeschwader 2 for 'Jagdgeschwader Richtofen' worn on the lower right sleeve by all ranks. This was introduced in March 1935. (Phil Phillips Collection)

BELOW: This group of officers show a mix of dress, some wearing the *Fliegerbluse*, others the service uniform. The officer on the left is wearing breeches, while the officer with his back to the camera wears long trousers and shoes. He also has a white summer uniform cap. Note the cuff title on the right sleeve worn by the two on the left of the photo. (Chris Goss)

SERVICE DRESS

Britain was 'Jagdgeschwader Schlageter' named after Albert Leo Schlageter, a veteran of the First World War. The cuff title itself was of silver text embroidered onto a black background. It was worn by all officers, NCOs and men of Jagdgeschwader 26. One of its famous bearers was Adolf Galland who commanded Jagdgeschwader 26 from 22 August 1940 to 5 December 1941. Others included 'Jagdgeschwader Richtofen' which was Jagdgeschwader 132 then Jagdgeschwader 2.

Aiguillettes

These were mainly worn on the officers' and officials' right shoulder. They were in aluminium colour for ranks up to Oberst and in gold for generals. They were normally worn with parade dress, day or evening dress which was the service uniform tunic.

RIGHT: A set of matt silver aluminium dress aiguillettes as worn by all grades of Luftwaffe officers for full dress parade. (Simon Lannoy Collection)

Section 7
OTHER FLYING EQUIPMENT AND PAPERWORK

Aircrew were issued maps and flight computers to help with the safe conduct of operations from a flight planning perspective. Working out fuel consumption was a key factor for the Bf 109 crews and getting meteorological data such wind speed and direction along with exact distances scaled from the map would give an idea of loiter times over the target before they had to make their way home.

As always the equipment provided for the Luftwaffe is of good quality and well-marked, as can be seen by the pencils! As for logbooks, each member of crew would have been expected to keep a meticulous record of his sorties so they were issued with a card-backed basic log but many opted for leatherbound or hardback versions. Again the Luftwaffe *Soldbuch* shows the detail in which the Luftwaffe kept its records. Although the RAF had service/pay books they were not so detailed.

AIRCREW TIME PIECES

The Luftwaffe issued the large B-Uhren chronograph to navigators of heavy bombers but these had to be returned to stores after each flight. These large-faced pieces were 55mm across and had a large oversized leather strap to fit on the outside of the flying gear, and were made by a number of well-known watch companies such as A. Lange & Sohne, Wempe, Laco and Stowa. The fighter pilots, however, had the smaller-faced watches although again with an oversized strap made by Glasschute and Hanhart although the Hanhart was a private purchase option. Knowing the time and flight duration is critical to aviators and particularly fighter pilots. With such a high fuel consumption rate and limited fuel capacity, their time over England was quite limited so a cautious eye on the time with regards to available fuel left in the tanks to save a swim in the Channel was important.

Time is also important for navigation and a pilot would mark his map with heading and time for each leg if doing longer sorties. During the Battle of Britain the fighter pilots would brief before their flight on rendezvous positions with bombers and basic headings and timings only, as map reading

OTHER FLYING EQUIPMENT AND PAPERWORK

RIGHT: An example of the Bauart B later issue B-Uhr watch issued to navigators and crew of larger aircraft, the strap being large enough to wear on the outside of the flying suit or uniform, the first examples being introduced in 1939. This particular boxed example was made by Laco and is dated 1943. Fighter pilots often opted for smaller wristwatches such as the Hanhart. (Phil Phillips Collection)

ABOVE LEFT and RIGHT: An early single-push Hanhart 17 Jewel watch which was private purchase and favoured by the fighter pilots. This particular example dates to 1940. The leather strap is a modern replacement but of the type used on the original. (Simon Lannoy Collection)

THE LUFTWAFFE BATTLE OF BRITAIN FIGHTER PILOT'S KITBAG

was not normally required as they were escorting a bomber formation. In case of emergency or being separated the crews would have had an idea of headings to return to their home airfield.

FLIGHT COMPUTER

The flight computer issued to Luftwaffe aircrew was the DR2 known as the '*Knemyer*' by pilots but it is marked '*Dreieckrechner*' or 'triangle computer' which basically helps work out the triangle of velocities required for navigation, wind, airspeed and track. The calculating side can help work out true air speed, remaining fuel etc. The device did not change much from 1936 through the Battle of Britain period. Remaining fuel was always on the mind of the fighter pilot, especially when operating over the Channel as mentioned by Adolf Galland: 'During a single sortie of my group we lost twelve fighter planes, not by enemy action, but simply because after two hours flying time the bombers we were escorting had not yet reached the mainland on their return journey. Five of these fighters managed to make a pancake landing on the French shore with their last drop of fuel; seven of them landed in the "drink".'[20]

LEFT and BELOW: This is the front and rear of the *Dreieckrechner* DR2 flight computer, used to work out time/distance and headings, taking into account wind drift and magnetic variation. This particular example was manufactured in 1940. (Mark Hillier Collection)

OTHER FLYING EQUIPMENT AND PAPERWORK

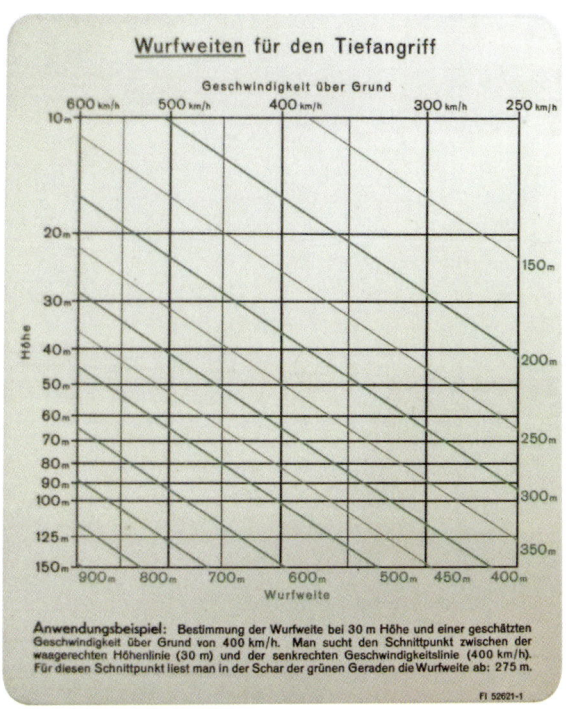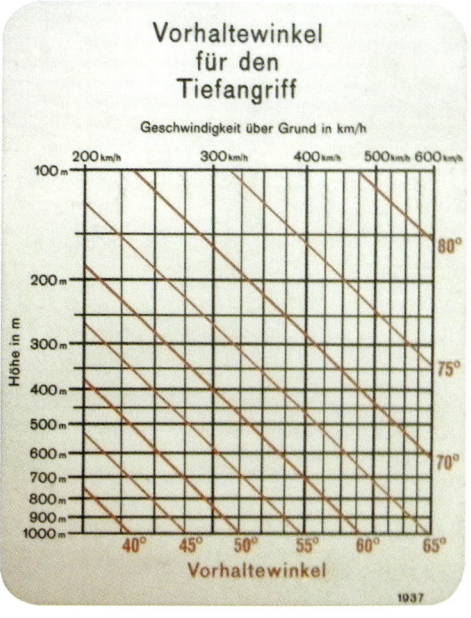

ABOVE: A calculator used for dive bombing dated 1937, the left for working out the throw and the right for angle. The top scale is for speed, the vertical scale for height. (Mick Prodger Collection)

GROUND STRAFING\DIVE BOMBING FLIGHT COMPUTER

Constructed from aluminium sheets, these were carried in the pocket of the flight suit and used in conjunction with the gunsight to calculate the correct speed, distance from target and altitude for ground strafing 'non-moving targets'. These are dated 1937 and one has printed text on one side the other on both with instructions for use and the issue part number FL 52621-1.

MAPS

Luftwaffe *Fliegerkarte* were often laminated paper, covered in celluloid so that they could be folded and used many times without ripping, often at a scale of 1:300,000 or 1:500,000 and which were always dated. Some of the maps were linen-backed, again for robustness and for repeated use. Early maps of the UK were just reproduced from the Ordnance Survey with an added translation for the key.

Often these maps will carry a unit number or squadron stamp. From various first-hand accounts it seems that some chose to fly with maps, but others felt that it was not necessary due to the short distance across the Channel, over water the maps were useless anyway and on a good day the coastlines and south of England were easy to make out from 15,000 feet and you knew where you were. The maps were also awkward to open in the cockpit and looking down at a map meant you were not keeping a good lookout for enemy fighters.

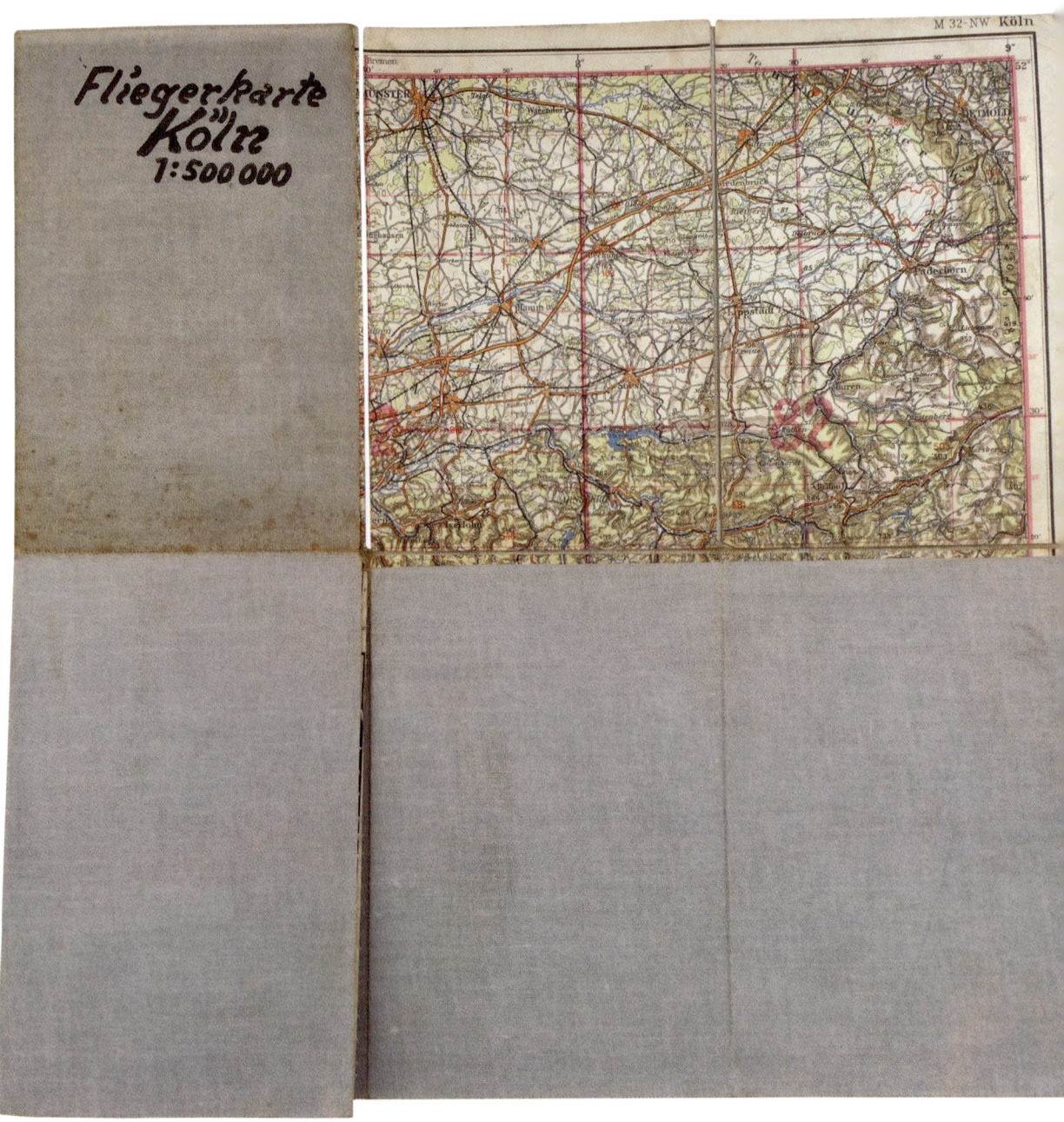

ABOVE: A small linen-backed map at a scale of 1:500,000 of the Koln area, marked *fligerkarte* and dated 1939. At this size and scale it is small enough to use in a fighter cockpit and could be tucked in a pocket, boot or under a harness strap. (Mark Hillier Collection)

OPPOSITE: A much larger-scale map again backed in linen, this time covering the whole of the north of Germany and up to the coastal areas. The map was used by 5/Kampfgeschwader 255 who operated the Do 17. This unit later changed to 8/Kampfgeschwader 77 which took part in the Battle of France and the Battle of Britain. (Mark Hillier Collection)

THE LUFTWAFFE BATTLE OF BRITAIN FIGHTER PILOT'S KITBAG

ABOVE: Seen here sat on his Bf 109 this Unteroffizier carries a small-scale map or extract in his boot, an ideal place to carry it. Note he has a flare bandolier around the top of the twin-zip black leather and suede boots. This photo is of Unteroffizier Karl Nowak of 9/Jagdgeschwader 2 taken in 1942 but is a classic fighter pilot look. (Chris Goss)

FABER NUMBER 3 PENCILS

Number 3 pencils seen here unsharpened and unused, still wrapped in paper with string and card insert dividers as they would have been. Red finish and marked '*Eigentum der Luftwaffe*' (Property of the Luftwaffe). This type was used by navigators, pilots, office staff and everyone else. Many official documents were filled out in pencil, including logbooks, so that errors could be more easily corrected.

OTHER FLYING EQUIPMENT AND PAPERWORK

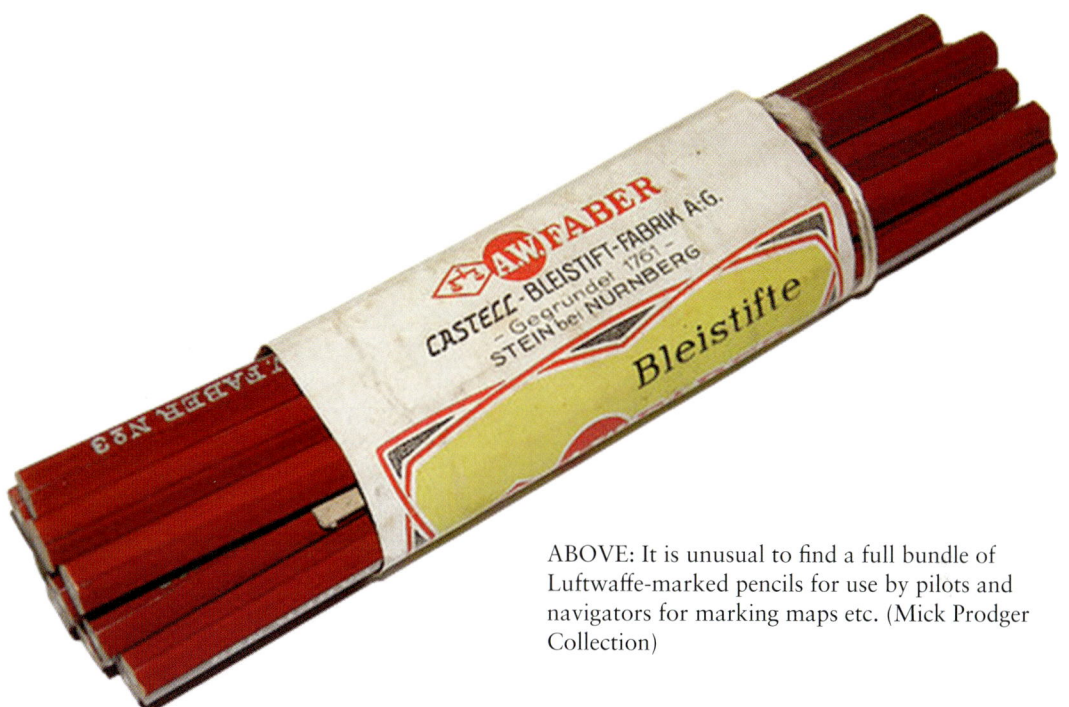

ABOVE: It is unusual to find a full bundle of Luftwaffe-marked pencils for use by pilots and navigators for marking maps etc. (Mick Prodger Collection)

LOGBOOK

The Luftwaffe issued all aircrew a *Flugbuch* within which would be recorded the details of each flight, date, hours flown, aircraft type and where the flight was from and too with details of the sortie. Some pilots chose to purchase leather-bound or hardback books with the National Emblem on the front. The issue variety had a soft cover with either a blue or orange front with *Flugbuch* on it. The details, rank and service number of the individual can normally be found inside the front cover on the hardbound versions and on the cover page on the softback version.

ABOVE: The cover of the Battle of Britain Luftwaffe fighter pilot's logbook which was the property of Karl Heinz Willhelm who flew the Bf 109 with III\Jagdgescwader 77 on. Note the black leather effect cover with gold leaf embossed national emblem, but after the war the swastika was scrubbed out. (Mark Hillier Collection)

127

THE LUFTWAFFE BATTLE OF BRITAIN FIGHTER PILOT'S KITBAG

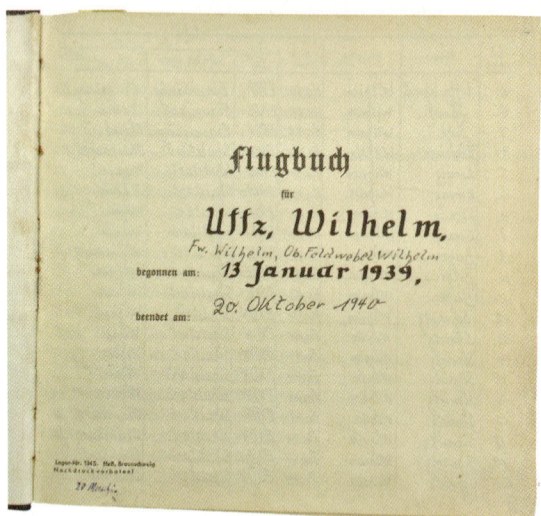

ABOVE: The last entry in his logbook can be seen in this photo. Note that the entries state *'frontflug'* or flying at the front, he was based at Marquise in France at the time of his final flight. He was flying Bf 109 Yellow 11 at the time he was shot down on 20 October 1940. The entry at the end of the line states 'on a flight over England he did not return'. (Mark Hillier Collection)

LEFT: The inside first page gives the details of the holder, including rank and name, start and end date. Willhelm learned to fly in 1939 and was shot down on 20 October 1940. He managed to bail out of his stricken Bf 109 and was taken prisoner. (Mark Hillier Collection)

LEFT: The front of the pilot's log book of Unteroffizier Ernst Braun. A Messerschmitt Bf 109 pilot of 6 Staffel JG26, Braun flew throughout the Battle of Britain, undertaking a number of sorties over Kent and Sussex during August 1940, until he was shot down and taken prisoner following combat over Shakespeare Cliff, Dover, on 7 September 1940. (Mark Hillier Collection)

OTHER FLYING EQUIPMENT AND PAPERWORK

ABOVE: A double-page spread from Unteroffizier Braun's logbook. Note the Spitfire he claimed in one of the 24 August entries. (Mark Hillier Collection)

Lfd. Nr. des Fluges	Führer	Begleiter	Muster	Zulassungs-Nr.	Zweck des Fluges	Abflug Ort
146	Braun		Bf 109	1937	Überprüfung	Marquise
47	"		"	735	"	"
48	"		"	60	Feindflug	"
149	"		"	61	"	"

Flug		Landung			Flugdauer	Kilometer	Bemerkungen
Tag	Tageszeit	Ort	Tag	Tageszeit			
6.9.	15.55	Marquise		16.30	35		
7.9.	9.35	"		9.55	20		
"	11.35	"		12.58	83		Angriff zu 88 nach London. Rest K.F.
"	18.00	"		/	/		Abgeschossen. Mit Fallschirm abgesprungen

Für die Richtigkeit der Flüge von
Lfd. Nr. 37 bis 149
bescheinigt:
Schneider
Oblt. u. Staffelkapitän z.b.

ABOVE: A further two pages of Unteroffizier Braun's logbook. This has the entry confirming that he was shot down and taken prisoner on 7 September 1940. (Mark Hillier Collection)

OTHER FLYING EQUIPMENT AND PAPERWORK

SOLDBUCH AND WEHRPASS

The Luftwaffe *Soldbuch* was a pay book and identity card and was issued to all Luftwaffe crews. It contained service and personal information along with details of training, qualifications and units served in as well as awards gained and was always carried by the individual. Made of thin cardboard, it could be either dark blue, light blue or grey in colour. The front cover would have on

ABOVE: The front cover of a *Wehrpass* showing the national emblem, the front stamped 'Luftwaffe'. This book was the property of an Obergefreiter of Kampfgeschwader 27 'Boelcke', a Luftwaffe medium bomber wing which flew during the Battle of Britain. (Phil Phillips Collection)

THE LUFTWAFFE BATTLE OF BRITAIN FIGHTER PILOT'S KITBAG

ABOVE: A view of interior pages of the *Wehrpass* which includes the photograph of the holder. (Phil Phillips Collection)

it the Luftwaffe Eagle rather than the National Emblem. These were not required to be carried on operations by aircrew. The *Wehrpass* was a fuller military service booklet. The front had the National Emblem but was stamped 'Luftwaffe' and was retained back at the main unit.

HANDBOOK OF THE LUFTWAFFE

Just like the RAF the Luftwaffe produced a basic handbook for all Luftwaffe recruits, the title of which translated as 'the teachings of the air force'. This paperback showed background, previous commanders and heroes, uniform, kit issue, inspection of kit and how to hang it in your wardrobe, basic hygiene, guard duty, uniforms, rank, sidearms and rifles as well as how to use a gas mask. A very useful little guide.

ABOVE: A well-thumbed copy of the Handbook of the Luftwaffe dated 1937–8, giving a whole range of basic essential information for the new recruit. (Mark Hillier Collection)

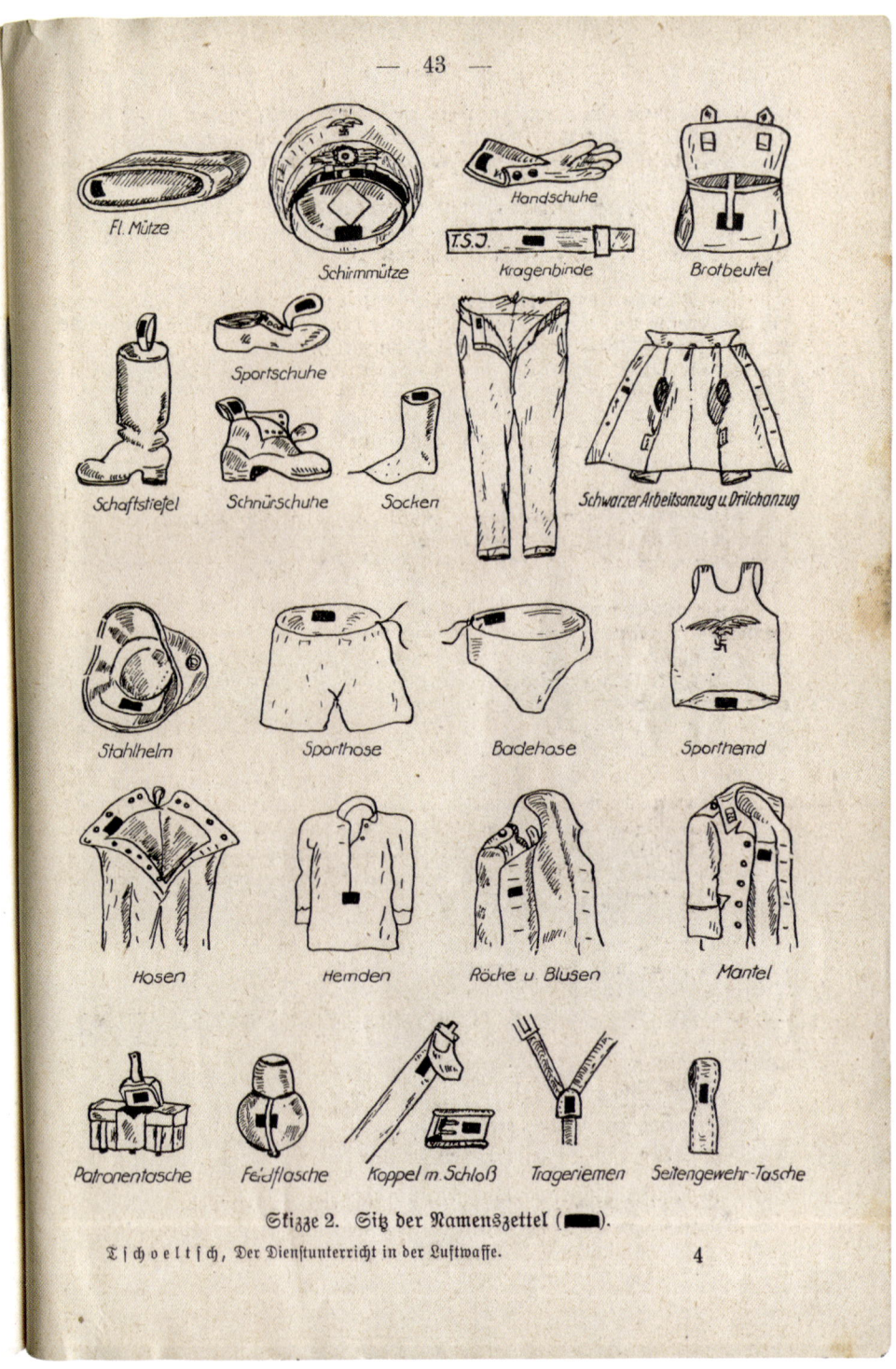

ABOVE: A page from the Handbook of the Luftwaffe showing basic kit issued to the new recruit. (Mark Hillier Collection)

OTHER FLYING EQUIPMENT AND PAPERWORK

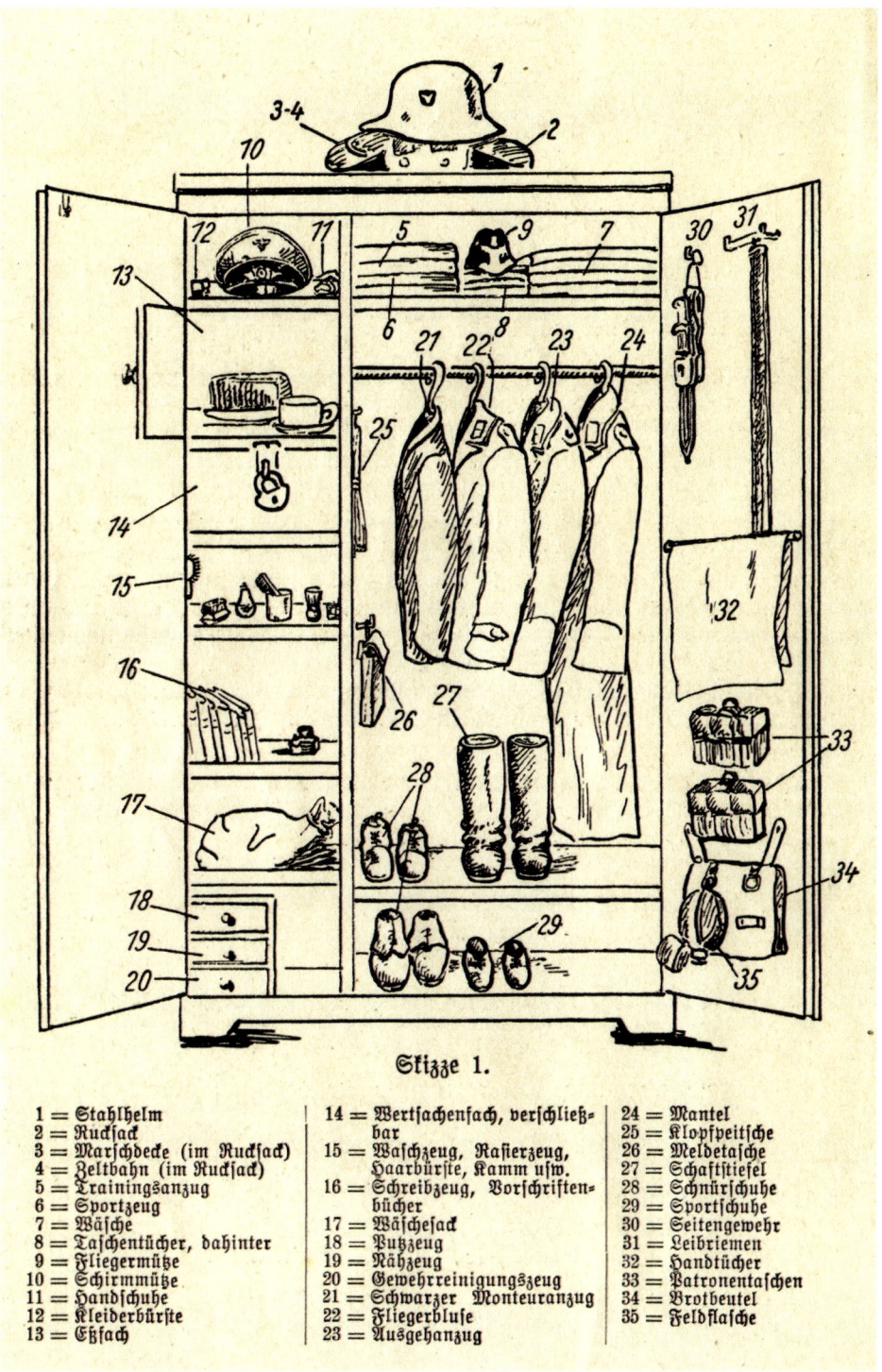

ABOVE: An illustration informing the Luftwaffe recruit on the correct manner of hanging his equipment in a wardrobe ready for kit inspection. (Mark Hillier Collection)

REFERENCES

1. Goss, Chris, *The Luftwaffe Fighters, Battle of Britain, The Inside Story: July-October 1940* (Crecy Publishing Ltd, Manchester, 2000), p.91.
2. Steinhilper, Ulrich, and Peter Osborne, *Spitfire on My Tail, a View from the Other Side* (Independent Books, Bromley, 1990), p.303.
3. Goss, p.66.
4. Ibid., p.158.
5. Ibid., p. 87.
6. Ibid., p.105.
7. Ibid., p.41.
8. Steinhilper and Osborne, p.232.
9. Goss, p.23.
10. Ibid., pp. 109,110.
11. Galland, Adolf, *The First and Last* (Methuen & Co Ltd, London, 1955), p.24.
12. Goss, p.181.
13. Ibid., p.91.
14. Ibid., p.118.
15. Ibid., p.77.
16. Ibid., p.90.
17. Ibid., p.119.
18. Ibid, p.187.
19. Ibid., p.41.
20. Galland, p.63.

BIBLIOGRAPHY

Bender, James Roger, *Air Organisations of the Third Reich* (D-D Associates, California, 1972).

Cano, Gustav and Santiago Guillen, *Deutsche Luftwaffe, Uniforms and Equipment of the German Air Force (1939-1945)* (Andrea Press, Madrid, 2013).

Davis, Brian L., *Luftwaffe Air Crews Battle of Britain 1940* (Arco Publishing Company, New York, 1974).

_____, *Uniforms and Insignia of the Luftwaffe, Volume 1: 1933-1940* (Arms and Armour, A Cassell Imprint, London, 1991).

_____, *Uniforms and Insignia of the Luftwaffe, Volume 2: 1940-1945* (Arms and Armour, A Cassell Imprint, London, 1995).

Galland, Adolf, *The First and Last* (Methuen & Co Ltd, London, 1955).

Goss, Chris, *The Luftwaffe Fighters, Battle of Britain, The Inside Story: July-October 1940* (Crecy Publishing Ltd, Manchester, 2000).

Philpott, Bryan, *German Fighters Over England* (Patrick Stephens Ltd, Cambridge, 1979).

Prodger, Mick J., *Vintage Flying Helmets, Aviation Headgear Before The Jet Age* (Schiffer Publishing Ltd, USA, 1995).

_____, *Luftwaffe vs RAF Flying Clothing of The Air War, 1939-45* (Schiffer Publishing Ltd, USA, 1997).

_____, *Luftwaffe vs RAF Flying Equipment of The Air War, 1939-45* (Schiffer Publishing Ltd, USA, 1998).

Steinhilper, Ulrich, and Peter Osborne, *Spitfire on My Tail, a View from the Other Side* (Independent Books, Bromley, 1990).